fixit

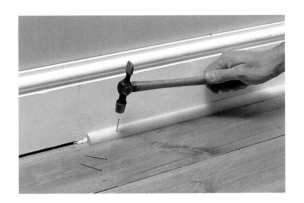

D1402073

fixit

Essential home maintenance and repairs,
from walls and windows to paving and brickwork

Consultant

John McGowan

Authors

Mike Collins, David Holloway, Brenda Legge, Diane Carr

Special Photography

Colin Bowling

southwater

This edition is published by Southwater

Southwater is an imprint of Anness Publishing Ltd
Hermes House, 88–89 Blackfriars Road, London SE1 8HA
tel. 020 7401 2077; fax 020 7633 9499
www.southwaterbooks.com; info@anness.com

© Anness Publishing Ltd 2003

This edition distributed in the UK by The Manning Partnership Ltd
6 The Old Dairy, Melcombe Road, Bath BA2 3LR
tel. 01225 478 444; fax 01225 478 440; sales@manning-partnership.co.uk

This edition distributed in the USA and Canada by National Book Network
4720 Boston Way, Lanham, MD 20706
tel. 301 459 3366; fax 301 459 1705; www.nbnbooks.com

This edition distributed in Australia by Pan Macmillan Australia
Level 18, St Martins Tower, 31 Market St, Sydney, NSW 2000
tel. 1300 135 113; fax 1300 135 103; customer.service@macmillan.com.au

This edition distributed in New Zealand by The Five Mile Press (NZ) Ltd
PO Box 33–1071 Takapuna, Unit 11/101–111 Diana Drive, Glenfield, Auckland 10
tel. (09) 444 4144; fax (09) 444 4518; fivemilenz@clear.net.nz

All rights reserved. No part of this publication may be reproduced, stored in a retrieval
system, or transmitted in any way or by any means, electronic, mechanical, photocopying,
recording or otherwise, without the prior written permission of the copyright holder.

A CIP catalogue record for this book is available from the British Library.

Publisher: Joanna Lorenz
Managing editor: Judith Simons
Project editor: Felicity Forster
Editor: Ian Penberthy
Designer: Paul Calver
Illustrator: Peter Bull
Photographer: Colin Bowling
Photography consultant: Simon Gilham
Technical assistant: John Ireland
Production controller: Claire Rae

Previously published as part of a
larger volume, *Do-It-Yourself.*

1 3 5 7 9 10 8 6 4 2

Publisher's note
The authors and the publisher have made every effort to ensure that all instructions contained in this book are accurate
and safe, and cannot accept liability for any resulting injury, damage or loss to persons or property, however it may arise.
If in doubt as to the correct procedure to follow for any home improvements task, seek professional advice.

642.7
F566

Contents

NOV 1 3 2003
GERMANTOWN COMMUNITY LIBRARY
GERMANTOWN, WI 53022

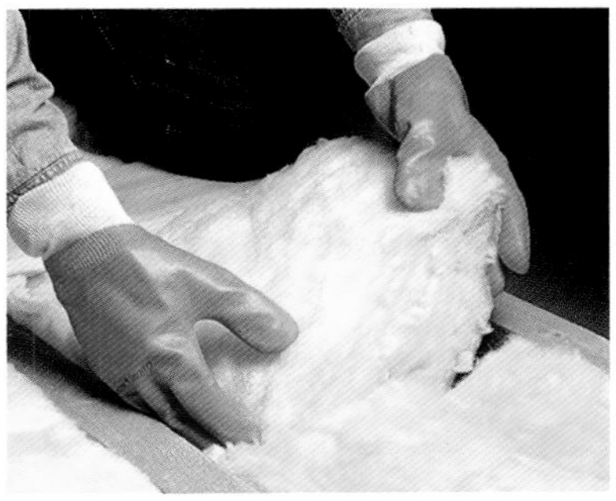

INTRODUCTION

Almost certainly, your home will be the most valuable asset you possess, and it pays to look after your investment. Regular maintenance is essential, and from time to time you will also need to make repairs, both inside and out. Whether fixing a fence or something far more ambitious, the same approach to the work is needed – the whole job must be planned thoroughly if you want a good result.

IMMEDIATE ACTION

Whether you live in a house or apartment, a converted barn or tiny studio, the structure of your home will be subjected to constant wear and tear, both indoors and out, and no matter how well you look after it, sooner or later something will work loose, warp, crack, crumble or break. When that happens, you must waste no time in putting matters right; invariably, delay will make the problem worse, and the solution could be costly. Moreover, before you can carry out even the most basic of do-it-yourself tasks – painting or papering a wall perhaps – you must make sure that surfaces are sound and in good condition to ensure the best result.

CONSTANT ATTACK

Many indoor repairs become necessary through the simple day-to-day use of your home. The

LEFT Even the most well-cared-for of homes can need repairs from time to time. The entire structure is at risk of damage, and timely intervention is essential to prevent small problems from becoming large, costly ones.

regular opening and closing of windows and doors, for example, will take its toll on hinges and catches, and even on their frames, which can work loose or twist. Then, of course, glass is easily broken. Wood is a major structural constituent of all homes, but it can flex under load and it is affected by the amount of moisture in the air, leading to cracking and warping. In certain conditions, it's also prone to attack by wet or dry rot, fungus and woodworm, all of which can weaken it severely. Even hard

LEFT Choosing and using the right materials and equipment for the job is vital.

surfaces like plaster walls and ceilings, exposed masonry and concrete or tiled floors are not immune from damage. Cracks may appear through building settlement and damage may be done accidentally by dropping heavy objects on them.

Outdoors, similar problems apply, but are exacerbated by the constant action of the weather. Hot sun, driving rain, strong winds and icy temperatures all have an adverse effect on the structure of your home and its surroundings. If ignored, any damage could allow the weather to penetrate to the interior, with serious consequences.

Fortunately, much of the repair work you are likely to face is not beyond the abilities of anyone with a practical turn of mind who is prepared to make the effort to learn the necessary skills. This book will show you how to make a wide variety of repairs and achieve professional results, thus saving you money and giving you a useful skill into the bargain. Being able to exercise a skill is an enriching experience that adds to the fullness of life, especially so if your working time is normally spent in an academic or sedentary job. There is also the pure pleasure that goes with learning and using a new skill successfully. Even if you feel that some jobs are beyond you, knowing how they are done will be of great help when employing a professional.

Hidden benefits

The money saved in carrying out your own repair work is an obvious advantage and, in a healthy property market, can help create an asset that will grow over the years. Furthermore, for many people, the physical nature of do-it-yourself gives much-needed exercise in the evenings or weekends, which is all important for a healthy lifestyle. Knocking-up concrete, planing wood or climbing up and down ladders all contribute to keeping us in trim.

Gaining experience

Specialized skills, such as bricklaying and carpentry, do need the experience of actually handling the tools and materials regularly to gain manual dexterity, and the best way to obtain this experience is to do a few outdoor jobs that are not particularly important. Repairing a fence or wall, or perhaps re-laying a few paving slabs will help you develop skills remarkably quickly and boost your confidence.

Beginners should seek as much advice as possible from experienced professionals, or at least read up on the relevant repair so that the more common pitfalls can be avoided. Many colleges offer evening classes where, for a modest sum, the novice can learn carpentry, brickwork and a variety of general do-it-yourself skills. These are worth investigating and can be very rewarding. A final advantage of

ABOVE FAR LEFT Plastering a whole wall requires a lot of skill, but it is easier to do smaller repairs where needed.

ABOVE LEFT Basic carpentry skills can be put to good use by fixing a garden gate.

ABOVE Bricklaying and pointing skills take practice and time to learn properly.

BELOW Virtually any floorcovering can be laid perfectly if the sub-floor is well prepared.

doing your own repair work is that your time is free, so never rush a job; haste encourages mistakes, which leads to disappointment and can be expensive in the cost of replacing spoiled materials.

PLANNING

The hardest part of any do-it-yourself project is deciding precisely what you want and planning how to achieve it. The decisions may involve simply choosing a colour scheme, or may be more complex, perhaps involving major changes to style, layout of a room, features and fittings. The secret of success is careful preparation, an understanding of basic colour scheming, and learning how to make the best use of the wide range of tools and materials available to the do-it-yourself enthusiast.

FORWARD PLANNING

Planning ahead is an essential ingredient of successful projects. It is important to remember that some schemes may involve a room or rooms being out of bounds for some days or even weeks, and provision must be made for this. Similarly, it is generally wiser to schedule the painting of the outside of your property for the summer months when there is at least a likelihood of good weather.

INFRASTRUCTURE

There is little point in decorating any part of the house if you envisage having it rewired in the near future, or perhaps adding central heating. These major domestic services will need to be installed first. If you are planning an extension in a year or so, much the same will apply, so it is best to work out an overall scheme that considers major items.

BE PREPARED

It may be that at some point in a job you will need another pair of hands to hold or pass tools in an awkward spot, or to help with moving heavy objects. Just arranging for someone to be there at the right time can be a problem. When beginning a job such as decorating, be sure that everything is to hand; it is no use pasting wallpaper then finding that you are too short to reach the top of the wall to hang it and that you need to go looking for a trestle or a pair of steps. All these things must be well prepared and in position.

COSTS

Plenty of projects have failed through lack of funds, so it is well worth costing your job carefully. If the job is to be done in stages as the money becomes available, make sure that you can put it "on hold" without any detrimental effects. Stripping the paint from exterior woodwork then leaving it for months to absorb moisture is asking for trouble. Removing old windows before the new ones are actually on site is tempting the gods!

VIABILITY

This is the most important consideration of all. Viability not only covers whether a job can be done, but also whether it is beneficial to do it. Cladding good brickwork with stone, flush-panelling fine old panelled doors, and ripping out ornate skirting (base) boards will only detract from the value of your home, so if you live in a house with a particular architectural style, keep it that way.

ABOVE Keep the bulk of the exterior upkeep to do in the summer time.

BELOW LEFT Keep all your tools for the specific job near to hand.

BELOW All of these items will prove invaluable for drawing plans for your projects: graph paper; a sketch pad; a clipboard or drawing board; masking tape; a pair of compasses; dividers for the accurate transfer and duplication of measurements; drawing pens; pencils; eraser and pencil sharpener; a set square and protractor; templates for necessary shapes; rules; and a scale rule and a calculator for converting measurements and making calculations.

Use this checklist to help in organizing your do-it-yourself project and to draw up a record of the tools, equipment and materials that are required.

TASK	MATERIALS	TOOLS/EQUIPMENT
1 Remove furniture from affected room(s)		
2 Remove fixtures and fittings: go to 7 if not executing major work. Order new fixtures and fittings		
3 Relocate room contents		
4 Carry out structural alterations		
5 Alter/extend/improve services, e.g. improve wiring/plumbing		
6 Replace features that are to be altered such as doors, mouldings (trims)		
7 Remove old wall and floorcoverings if being replaced		
8 Make good any damaged surfaces		
9 Wash painted/ceiling surfaces, apply primer sealer as necessary		
10 Wash painted woodwork, clean room before starting to decorate		
11 Level and repair floors as necessary		
12 Replace fixtures and fittings, such as light switches		
13 Fix wall tiles, cladding or panelling		
14 Paint or paper ceilings		
15 Paint or paper walls		
16 Paint woodwork (if papering walls, do this first)		
17 Add decorative moulding (trim), borders etc		
18 Replace shelf brackets, curtain (drapery) track, built-in furniture		
19 Lay new floorcoverings and clean room		
20 Reposition furniture		
21 Add soft furnishings		

USING PROFESSIONALS

A do-it-yourself project can be as simple as hanging a picture or putting up a shelf, or as complex as creating a new room in the roof. In extreme cases, it can even mean building a full-scale house. Most of us do not go that far, but there are many jobs, especially in plumbing and electrics, where professional help is welcome and indeed necessary.

REGULATIONS

Some projects require professional input by law, such as when local planning (zoning) permission is required or, more commonly, when the work must comply with building regulations. In this case, when applications must be made to a local authority, it is well worth securing the services of an architect, or at least a professional draughtsman, to draw up plans. He or she will be familiar with the building regulations of the local area and almost certainly will save you time and money in presenting the plans effectively to the right people.

Perhaps, more importantly, such a professional can advise you in advance if your project is likely to fail for a reason you may not even have considered.

HANDS ON

As a do-it-yourself enthusiast, you have to be familiar with several trades, but it is often well worth employing a professional for structural work to save time and possibly money. For example, a small extension to your home could be brick-built with the roof put on and tiled in a few weeks, which would leave you plenty of time to have the wiring installed, then plaster the walls, make all secondary fixings such as floors, doors, skirting (base) boards and to decorate the extension in relative comfort.

You also have to remember that many aspects of building work require stamina and strength on the part of the operative. Digging a foundation trench is not ideal for someone not used to a physical challenge, indeed, it could lead to back problems or other injuries. Jobs such as carrying bricks or blocks up a ladder or moving concrete around are tough going. Even working in unfavourable weather conditions and without the necessary clothing may lead to health problems.

Many building jobs require specialist equipment that a builder will supply – for example, an excavator, concrete mixer, roof ladder, scaffolding, and so on. If you take on jobs that require this type of apparatus, then you will have to pay for them, either by hiring or buying.

BELOW LEFT A competent builder will construct a block or brick wall quickly and efficiently.

BELOW Hacking off defective plaster is a time-consuming and strenuous job for the beginner.

LEVELS OF COMPETENCE

Being able to run pipes and electrical cables is a very different matter from knowing what is necessary in the way of safety or operational and building regulations. Understanding the capacity requirements of pumps and fuses together with a wide range of other knowledge is absolutely necessary to ensure that installations work and are safe.

Incorrectly installed plumbing and electrical systems can produce potentially disastrous, even fatal, results. Therefore, employing an advisor to oversee these requirements is essential if you have the slightest doubt about your own ability. Indeed, in many countries, it is a legal requirement that all such work is carried out by licensed tradespeople. Many contractors will offer advice for a small fee.

It can be very costly in terms of both time and money if plumbing or electrics are incorrectly installed and have to be taken out and done again.

CHOOSING HELP

Recommendations by word of mouth in the building trade are paramount and are especially valuable if the contractor you choose not only works, but also lives in your local area. Ask for the addresses of jobs the contractor has done recently in the area and make arrangements to go and see them – it is the best recommendation of all.

When you have made a shortlist of likely builders or contractors (at least three is usual) ask each of them for an estimate cost for the work to be done. Make sure that each has the same, detailed list of the jobs involved. When you have decided on the one to use (never automatically opt for the cheapest – consider all the relevant factors), ask for a firm quotation for the work.

When you have chosen your builder, plumber or electrician, then go through the whole job with him or her and get all the decisions in writing, which can save disputes later on.

PRACTICAL TIPS

• When you are employing a builder, carpenter, plumber or electrician, get a clear, written agreement on the method of payment. Some builders will complete a job before seeking payment, others will ask for stage payments.

• Always agree, before any work starts, that you will withhold a proportion of the costs (5–10 per cent is usual) for an agreed period of time after the job is finished. This will cover any snagging or work that has to be done again through faulty workmanship or materials.

• If you decide to make concrete yourself, consider buying a second-hand concrete mixer, and selling it again when the job is complete – it should save you money on buying or hiring costs.

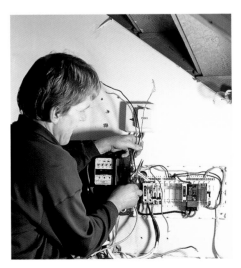

ABOVE Employ a qualified electrician to carry out electrical work, as incorrectly installed electrics can be lethal. At least, get a qualified person to check out your work.

ABOVE Approach every job methodically. When decorating a room, clear it completely if possible. Check that all necessary equipment and materials are to hand.

ABOVE Whereas a builder is often able to work by him or herself, the do-it-yourself enthusiast will on occasions have to get a helper. It requires special handling skills to work alone.

Safety Equipment

A complete book could be devoted to the subject of safety in the home, and there is a wide range of equipment designed to minimize our capacity for hurting ourselves. Nevertheless, there is one requirement that we cannot buy, without which all that equipment is virtually useless, namely concentration. This is particularly important when working alone.

Awareness

Concentration is essential when using any form of power tool, especially a saw, where one slip can mean the loss of a finger, or worse. The dangers of accidents involving electricity are well documented, as are those involving falls from ladders, spillages of toxic materials, and burns and injuries caused by contact with fire or abrasive surfaces. In almost every case, there is a loss of concentration, coupled with poor work practices and inadequate protective clothing or equipment. So, although the items shown here are all useful, concentrating on what you are doing is the best advice to prevent accidents from occurring around the home and workshop.

ABOVE Rubber knee pads for floor work avoid damage to both the floor and person.

LEFT The "bump" cap is more stylish than the hard hat and will cope with most accidents.

Basic equipment

Overalls are a good investment because they not only protect clothing, but also most are designed to be close-fitting to prevent accidental contact with moving machinery. Industrial gloves, although not worn by those engaged in fine work, can provide very useful protection against cuts and bruises when doing rougher jobs, such as fencing and garden work. Similarly, safety boots should be worn when heavy lifting or the use of machinery is involved. They are essential when using a chainsaw.

Knee pads are necessary for comfort when laying a floor, stripping one for varnishing or carrying out any other job that requires a lot of kneeling. They will also protect the wearer from injury if a nail or similar projection is knelt on accidentally. Finally, a bump cap is worth considering. This will protect the head from minor

FAR LEFT Wear overalls for protection when painting and decorating.

ABOVE LEFT Gloves are essential when handling rough materials.

LEFT Safety boots with steel toe caps will protect your feet.

injuries and bumps, but is not so cumbersome as the hard hat required on building sites.

It is inevitable that minor cuts and abrasions will occur at some point so a basic first aid kit is another essential for the home or workshop.

AIRBORNE DANGERS

When you are working with wood, the most common airborne danger is dust, mainly from sawing and sanding. This can do long-term damage to the lungs. Many do-it-yourself enthusiasts do not do enough work to warrant a workshop dust extractor, but it would be worth considering if funds allowed. Such a device can be wall-mounted or portable. In the latter case, it can be moved around the house or workshop to suit any tool in use.

A simple face mask, however, will offer adequate protection for occasional jobs. These can also be purchased for protection against fumes, such as from solvents, which can be very harmful. Dust, of course, also affects the eyes, so it is worth investing in a pair of impact-resistant goggles, which will protect the wearer from both fine dust and

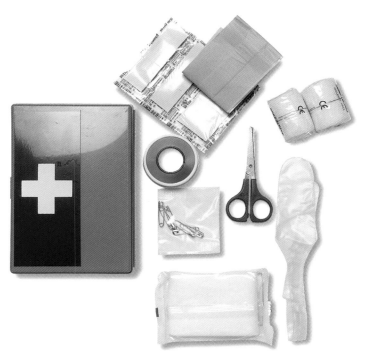

LEFT Keeping a basic first aid kit is a common and wise precaution even before any do-it-yourself work is envisaged. It should always be prominently displayed for people unfamiliar with the workshop.

flying debris. Full facial protection is available in the form of a powered respirator for those working in dusty conditions over long periods.

Excessive noise is another airborne pollutant that can be dangerous over a long period. Woodworking machinery, such as planers and circular saws, is often the culprit. Earplugs are the simplest solution and can be left in the ears over a long period. If you need to be able to hear between short bouts of working, ear protectors are the

answer. These can be worn in conjunction with other facial protection quite easily.

PRACTICAL TIP

• Perhaps the most basic advice is to never work alone with machinery and if it is possible always have a friend or colleague nearby to help. If there is no telephone, having a mobile (cell) phone is handy in the workshop.

ABOVE Ear defenders are good for really loud noise but should be used sparingly.

ABOVE Dust extraction is the first line of defence in the workshop.

ABOVE A simple face mask can filter out the worst dust pollution.

ELECTRICAL AND LADDER SAFETY

Most safety considerations concerning the use of power tools will be set out by the manufacturers in the operating instructions, so it is essential always to read the manuals on purchase and follow these to the letter. Using ladders, however, needs some direct input from the user by way of common sense, since no two situations are ever the same.

ELECTRICAL SAFETY

Some tools have removable switches that allow the user to immobilize the tool and prevent any unauthorized use. Provisions for the use of padlocks are also common on machinery, and it is wise to buy tools with such facilities.

To safeguard against electrocution, which can occur if the flex (power cord) is faulty or is cut accidentally, the ideal precaution is a residual current device (RCD). This is simply plugged into the main supply socket (electrical outlet) before the flex and will give complete protection to the user. Extension leads (power cords) can be purchased with automatic safety cut-outs and insulated sockets and are ideal for both outside and inside work.

The danger of electrocution or damage caused by accidentally drilling into an existing cable or pipe can be largely prevented by using an electronic pipe and cable detector, which will locate and differentiate between metal pipes, wooden studs and live wires through plaster or concrete to a depth of approximately 50mm (2in). These are not too expensive and will be very useful around the home.

The danger of fire is ever present in both the home and workshop, so a fire extinguisher (possibly two or three) is necessary for every do-it-yourself enthusiast. It should be wall-mounted in plain view and tested and serviced regularly.

ABOVE AND LEFT Pipe and cable detectors give information which can largely eliminate any danger from electrocution.

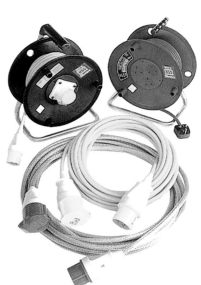

ABOVE Proper cable reels and insulated sockets protect the user from electrocution.

ABOVE A fire extinguisher is absolutely essential in the workshop or at home. Make sure the one you have is adequate for the size and type of workshop, and the type of fire source.

LEFT A simple circuit breaker can save a life.

ABOVE A ladder platform will ensure a firm footing, especially if heavy footwear is worn.

SLIPPING AND FALLING

Steps and ladders can be hazardous, so make sure they are in good condition. Accessories to make a ladder safer to use include the roof hook, which slips over the ridge for safety; the ladder stay, which spreads the weight of the ladder across a vertical surface, such as a wall to prevent slippage; and the standing platform, which is used to provide a more comfortable and safer surface to stand on. The last often has a ribbed rubber surface and can be attached to the rungs of almost all ladders. Even more stable is the moveable workstation or a board or staging slung between two pairs of steps or trestles. These can often be used with a safety rail, which prevents the operator from falling even if a slip occurs.

ABOVE RIGHT A moveable workstation simplifies the whole process.

RIGHT Platforms supported by trestles are the safest way to paint from a height.

RIGHT Keeping tools on a stable surface when working at heights adds to your personal safety.

BELOW RIGHT A ladder attachment over the ridge of a roof improves safety and avoids damage to the roof covering.

BELOW Make sure that your ladder is secure at ground level. This is one of the most important steps to safe working practice.

PRACTICAL TIPS

• Never over-reach when working on steps or a ladder; climb down and reposition it.

• Never allow children or pets into areas where power tools or strong solvents are being used.

• Do not work when you are overtired. This causes lapses in concentration, which can lead to silly and/or dangerous mistakes.

• Keep the work environment tidy. Flexes (power cords) should not be walked on or coiled up tightly, because it damages them internally. Moreover, trailing flexes can be a trip hazard and long extension leads (cords) can be prone to overheating.

Maintenance and Repairs

Where your home is concerned, prevention is often better, and certainly less expensive, than cure. A regular programme of inspection and maintenance will prevent small problems from becoming large and expensive ones. From time to time, however, repairs will be necessary, and their successful completion depends on having all the necessary tools and equipment to hand, and understanding how to use them.

REPAIRING AND REPLACING FLOORBOARDS

The majority of floors in older homes will have individual floorboards nailed to floor joists. In modern homes, sheets of flooring-grade chipboard (particle board) will be nailed or screwed to the joists. If a new floor covering is to be laid, it is essential that floors are in good condition. If floorboards are to be exposed, they need to be in even better condition, as any defects will be visible.

LIFTING FLOORBOARDS

To inspect the underfloor space or fit new floorboards, you will need to lift existing floorboards. You may find some that have been cut and lifted in the past to provide access to pipes or cables. These should be easy to lever up with the flat blade of a bolster (stonecutter's) chisel – do not use a screwdriver as you will damage the floorboard.

To lift boards that have not been cut, check first that they are not tongued-and-grooved – a tongue along one edge of each board fitting into a groove along the adjacent edge of its neighbour. If they are, use a floorboard saw or a circular saw with its cutting depth set to 20mm (¾in) to cut through the tongue.

Lever up the floorboard with your bolster chisel, and use a floorboard saw to make a right-angled cut across it. Make the cut exactly over a joist so that the two parts of the board will be supported when they are replaced.

REPAIRING JOISTS

ABOVE Cut the new joist section to length and clamp it in place while you drill holes through it and through the old joist.

Chipboard sheets are easy to unscrew, but you may need to cut through tongues in the same way as for traditional floorboards.

JOIST PROBLEMS

Most of the problems associated with floor joists are due to dampness, which may occur if airbricks (vents) have become blocked or if there are not enough airbricks to ensure adequate ventilation of the underfloor space.

ABOVE Pass bolts through the holes and add a washer before securing the nuts with a spanner.

Lift a few floorboards and inspect the joists with a torch and a mirror, prodding any suspect areas with a bradawl (awl). If sections of joist are damaged, you should be able to cut and lift floorboards or chipboard sheets over the damage and bolt on a new section of joist of the same size, making sure that it is fixed to solid wood. Do not bother to remove the old joist unless it is actually rotten. If you do find signs of dry rot (typically white strands), all damaged

REMOVING A SECTION OF FLOORBOARD

1 If it is a tongued-and-grooved board, cut through the tongue with a circular saw.

2 Lift the end of the floorboard by levering with a bolster (stonecutter's) chisel.

3 Wedge the board up and cut, over a joist, with a floorboard saw.

THE NATIONAL COMMUNITY LIBRARY
SHEBOYGAN, WI 53082

ABOVE Plane down floorboards if they are too wide to fill the gap.

ABOVE Use card or plywood packing pieces over the joists if the board is too shallow.

ABOVE Use a chisel to cut a slot to fit over a joist if the board is too thick.

wood must be removed by a firm of professionals. If you find signs of woodworm attack, treat the affected areas with a recommended woodworm eradicator or call in a professional firm.

LOOSE FLOORBOARDS

If floorboards are loose, the best answer is to replace the nails holding them down with screws. Do not put a screw in the middle of a board – there could be a pipe underneath. If nail heads are protruding, use a hammer and nail punch to set them below the surface of the floorboards. This is essential before attempting to use a sanding machine or laying carpet or sheet vinyl.

DAMAGED FLOORBOARDS

If floorboards are split or broken, the damaged section, at least, will need to be replaced. The most likely problem is that old floorboards will have become "cupped", or turned up at the edges. You can overcome this by hiring a floor sanding machine.

You do not need to replace a whole floorboard if only part of it is damaged; simply lift the board and cut out the damaged section, making the cuts over the centres of joists.

If replacement floorboard is too wide, plane it down to fit the gap – do not fit a narrower replacement floorboard, as you will get draughts. If the board is slightly thicker, chisel slots out of it where it fits over the joists; if it is thinner, use packing

pieces of cardboard or plywood between the joists and the board.

Secure each floorboard with two floorboard nails at each joist, positioning them about 25mm (1in) from the edge of the board and exactly in the middle of the joist. It is a good idea to drill nail pilot holes in the board first.

PRACTICAL TIP

• When laying new floorboards or new floor coverings, make sure that you can still gain access to pipes and cables underneath. If necessary, cut a removable inspection hatch in both the floor and the floor covering.

FIXING FLOORBOARDS

ABOVE Drill pilot holes for floorboard nails to avoid splitting the wood.

ABOVE Hammer down protruding nails to prevent them damaging the floor covering.

ABOVE Secure loose floorboards by replacing the nails with screws.

GERMANTOWN COMMUNITY LIBRARY
GERMANTOWN, WI 53022

REPAIRING CRACKS AND HOLES IN FLOORS

Before laying a new floorcovering, it is essential that the existing floor surface is sound and smooth. As well as repairing or replacing floorboards, you may have to fill cracks and holes in wooden floors, and deal with unevenness, and possibly damp, in solid floors. Any faults not rectified will eventually show through the floor covering and may damage it.

FILLING HOLES IN TIMBER FLOORS

Nail and screw holes can easily be plugged using a flexible wood filler applied with a filling or putty knife. If the floorboards are to be left exposed and treated with a clear sealer, try to match the wood filler, or stopping, to the colour of the surrounding floorboards – so do the filling after any sanding.

Larger recesses can also be filled with flexible filler, but if a knot has fallen out, leaving a large round hole, plug this by gluing in a short length of dowel and planing it smooth afterwards. Select a dowel that matches the colour of the floor or stain it once planed down.

FILLING CRACKS IN TIMBER FLOORS

You will find two main kinds of crack in timber floors: splits in the ends of the floorboards and gaps between the boards.

A split can often be cured by skew (toe) nailing – that is driving two nails through the end of the board at an angle toward the centre and down into the joist. As the nails are driven in, they should close up the split.

Gaps between floorboards are more difficult to deal with. If they are narrow, flexible wood filler will work, but for wider gaps, you must cut slivers of wood and glue them into place in the gaps. Once the glue has dried, plane or sand the slivers flush with the surrounding floor and stain to match if necessary.

If there are lots of wide gaps between floorboards, a better solution is to lift all the floorboards one by one, starting at one side of the room and working toward the other, and re-lay them tightly against one another. Floorboard clamps will help you do this, as they force a board against its neighbour while you nail or screw it down.

LEVELLING A WOODEN FLOOR

Individual rough patches on a timber floor can be sanded down by hand, which you should do after using filler, but where floorboards have become cupped or are heavily encrusted with old paint, grease and polish, the best move is to hire an industrial-type sanding machine and re-sand the floor. Begin with coarse abrasive and progress through to the fine grades, working across the floorboards at an angle. Finish off by working along the floorboards with fine abrasive. Hire an edging sander as well, unless you own a belt sander, because the floor sander will not sand right up to the skirting boards.

FIXING GAPS IN FLOORBOARDS

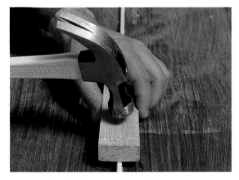

1 Drive glued slivers of wood between floorboards to fill large gaps.

2 Plane down the wood slivers flush with the floor when the glue has dried.

ABOVE Use flexible wood filler to cover the holes made by nail heads and screws.

ABOVE With a split board, first glue the split, then drive in nails at the end of the board.

1 Brush a crack in a solid floor with diluted PVA (white) glue to help new mortar bond to it.

2 Apply quick-set repair mortar to a crack in a solid floor. Level it flush and leave to harden.

3 If excessively porous, seal it by brushing on a coat of diluted PVA adhesive.

FILLING CRACKS AND HOLES IN SOLID FLOORS

Provided a solid floor is basically sound and dry, you should be able to fill cracks and holes using a quick set repair mortar. All loose material should be removed and the cracks enlarged if necessary to give the mortar something to grip.

The surface of the crack or hole should be brushed with a solution of one part PVA (white) adhesive and five parts water to reduce absorbency and help the mortar adhere to the floor. Use the same PVA adhesive and water solution to make up the mortar, then trowel it into place, building up two or more layers in a deep hole. Level the surface with a plasterer's trowel.

LEVELLING SOLID FLOORS

Little skill is required to produce a smooth, flat solid floor surface, as a self-levelling floor compound will do the job for you. Two types are available: both are powders and are mixed with either water or with a special latex emulsion.

Before you start, clear the room, removing all skirting (base) boards and doors; nail battens (furring strips) across thresholds to prevent the compound from spreading. Fill any cracks or holes more than 6mm (¼in) deep as described previously and brush the floor with the PVA/water solution. Mix the floor levelling compound in a bucket with water and tip it out on to the floor, spreading it out with a plasterer's trowel or a float. Leave it to settle. Once the compound has dried, at least 24 hours, you can refit the skirting boards and doors, but check that the latter will clear the higher floor when opened – you may need to trim a little off the bottoms.

LAYING A SELF-LEVELLING COMPOUND

1 Mix up self-levelling floor compound according to the manufacturer's instructions.

2 Starting from a corner farthest from the door, pour the compound on to the floor.

3 Using a plasterer's trowel, smooth the compound to a thickness of 3mm (⅛in).

REPAIRING DAMAGED FLOORCOVERINGS

Of all the types of floorcovering, tiled finishes can be the easiest to repair, since individual tiles can often be lifted and replaced. The way you do it depends on whether the tile is hard or soft and on how it has been secured to the floor. Even damaged carpet can be patched effectively, but care needs to be taken to avoid further damage to surrounding areas.

CERAMIC AND QUARRY TILES

These are among the most difficult tiles to replace, as first you will have to chip out the old tile. Drill a few holes in the tile with the biggest masonry drill you own, then use a club (spalling) hammer and cold chisel to chip out the tile, making sure you do not damage the surrounding tiles. Chip out all old adhesive or mortar from under the tile and grout from the edges.

Lay some new tile adhesive for ceramic tiles or mortar for quarry tiles and push the replacement tile gently into place. If it is not flush with its neighbours, lift it quickly and add or remove adhesive or mortar as necessary. Clean any excess mortar or adhesive off the face of the tile and leave to set before making good the gaps around the tile with grout for ceramic tiles or more mortar for quarry tiles. If re-laying several tiles, it helps if you make up some small spacers.

REPLACING A QUARRY TILE

1 Remove any cracked quarry (or ceramic) tiles with a club hammer and cold chisel.

2 Bed a new quarry tile on mortar, but use the recommended adhesive for ceramic tiles.

MOSAIC TIMBER TILES

There are two ways to replace these tiles. One is to lift the whole tile, which consists of four groups of timber strips, and replace with a new one. First drill or chisel out one strip and then lever the rest of the tile from the floor. The second method is to remove just the damaged strip or strips and glue in replacements taken from a spare tile, pressing them into place with a block of wood.

CARPET TILES

These are designed to be replaceable, so if you stain, burn or damage one in some other way, you have not ruined a whole carpet. Sometimes, the tile can simply be lifted and a new one put in its place, but some carpet tiles may be held down with double-sided adhesive tape, which will need replacing with the new tile – do not try to reuse any old tape.

REPLACING A MOSAIC STRIP

1 First drill a sequence of holes through the damaged mosaic strip.

2 Carefully cut away the strip around the holes with a chisel.

3 Apply a little glue to the new mosaic strip. Using a block of wood, hammer it in place.

Soft floor tiles

Most soft floor tiles – vinyl, cork, lino and rubber – are replaced in the same way. First you have to soften the adhesive holding the tile in place, which is best done with a hot-air gun, starting at one corner and gradually peeling the tile back. This becomes easier once you can direct the hot-air gun beneath the tile. An old chisel can be used to remove any remaining adhesive. Check that the replacement tile is an exact fit.

Some soft tiles are self-adhesive, requiring only the removal of backing paper, while others require a separate adhesive. Always add the adhesive to the back of a replacement tile to avoid staining the other tiles. With the adhesive in place, or the backing paper removed, hold the tile against the edge of one of the surrounding tiles and lower it into place. You may only get one attempt at this, so take care to get it right.

Carpet

Provided you have a matching piece, you can patch most types of carpet, but it may be worth cleaning the carpet first, since the patch may be a brighter colour. First decide how

1 Remove a vinyl or cork tile using a hot-air gun to soften the adhesive.

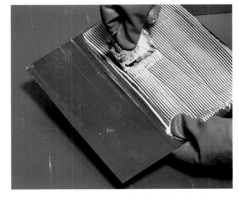

2 Apply adhesive to the back of the vinyl or cork tile and replace.

large the patch should be – if the carpet is patterned, you may want to join along a pattern line – cut the patch about 25mm (1in) larger than this all round, with the same part of any pattern. Lay the patch over the carpet, lining up the pattern exactly, and secure it with adhesive tape.

Using a trimming knife fitted with a new blade and a metal straightedge, make a single cut down through both thicknesses of carpet along each edge of the patch. Remove the tape and lift both pieces of carpet – the patch should fit exactly into the hole in the carpet with the pattern matching. With foam-backed carpet,

lay four strips of double-sided tape on the floor around the edges of the hole so that each strip overlaps the joint between the old carpet and the patch. Brush the edges of the patch and the hole with latex adhesive to prevent fraying, then press the carpet patch on to the tape. Remove excess adhesive with a damp cloth.

With fabric-backed carpet, use non-adhesive carpet repair tape and latex adhesive on the back and edges of the patch and the hole. Press the patch down into the hole with a wallpaper seam roller and wipe off any excess adhesive with a damp cloth.

Patching foam-backed carpet

1 Use a trimming knife and straightedge to cut through both the carpet patch and the existing carpet.

2 Press the carpet patch on to double-sided adhesive tape. Brush the edges with latex adhesive to prevent fraying.

3 The finished patch of carpet should fit exactly into the hole and the joins should be invisible in longer pile carpet.

Repairing Ceilings and Walls

Before carrying out any redecorating, such as painting or papering, ceilings and walls must be in near-perfect condition if the best results are to be achieved, as any defects will show through. This means filling any cracks, holes or other imperfections to leave a smooth surface. Fortunately, there is an excellent range of products for making good those defects.

Filling cracks

A general-purpose filler can be used for the majority of cracks in ceilings and walls. This comes ready-mixed in tubs or as a powder for mixing with water. The filler is simply applied with a filling or putty knife, pressing it into the cracks and smoothing it flush with the surface. Some cracks need enlarging slightly to give the filler something to grip; fine cracks can be filled with special hairline crack filler.

Normal fillers are quite adequate if you are papering the ceiling or wall, but for paint, a fine surface filler is better. Most fillers take a short while to dry, after which they can be sanded flush with the surrounding surface. Instant fillers set very quickly and are good for last-minute minor repairs while you are actually painting or papering.

Most of these fillers are equally as suitable for wood as for plaster – provided the wood is to be painted – so all your crack and small hole filling can be done in one go, using the same material. For cracks between two different materials, for example the wall plaster and timber architrave (trim) moulding around a door, use a flexible filler. This will absorb the inevitable movement between the two materials without opening up.

Filling holes

Small holes, especially those left by screws, can be filled in the same way as cracks. Cut off any protruding wall plugs or, better still, remove them altogether so that you can obtain a smooth finish.

Larger holes are more of a problem. The kind of hole left by removing a waste pipe from a wall can be made good with do-it-yourself repair plaster, which can usually be applied in layers up to 50mm (2in) thick. Smaller recesses up to 20mm (¾in) deep can be treated with a special deep-gap filler, while really deep cavities can be filled with an expanding foam filler. Once set, this can be cut and sanded smooth, then painted or papered over. If an area of plaster has fallen off the wall, use a repair plaster, levelling it with the surrounding sound plaster with a straight length of wood.

For larger areas, nail timber battens (furring strips) to the wall to act as guides for your timber straightedge.

Practical tip

• If you are repairing damage to a plastered external corner, pin a batten (furring strip) to one side of the corner to support the filler while it sets. For whole corners, use metal corner beading held in place with plaster.

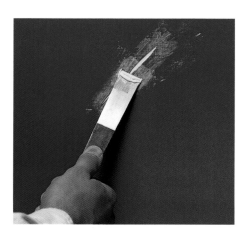

BELOW FAR LEFT Fill a fine crack with hairline crack filler, applied here with a putty knife.

BELOW LEFT Use a repair plaster for a deep hole, applied with a plasterer's trowel.

BELOW Use expanding foam filler to seal the gap around a window or door frame.

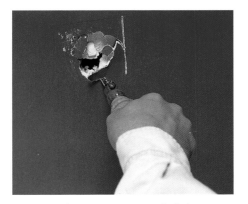

1 Use a padsaw to square up a hole in damaged plasterboard.

2 Attach a piece of string to the patch.

3 Butter the back of the patch with filler or coving adhesive.

REPAIRING PLASTERBOARD (GYPSUM BOARD)

Surface damage and small holes in plasterboard can be repaired in the same way as cracks and holes in solid plaster, but if a large hole has been punched in the material – by a door handle, say – a different solution is required. In this case, a patch must be placed behind the hole to provide support for a layer of filler.

First use a padsaw to open out the hole, squaring the sides. Then cut a section of fresh plasterboard to a length slightly less than the diagonal dimension of the hole. This will allow you to pass it through the hole at an angle. Drill a tiny hole in the middle of the plasterboard patch and insert a piece of knotted string through it before adding filler or coving (crown molding) adhesive to the edges on the grey side of the plasterboard. This will secure it firmly to the back of the existing plasterboard panel.

Pass the patch through the hole and pull it back against the edges. Hold the string taut while adding filler to the hole, then leave this to set. Cut off the projecting string and

4 Pass the plasterboard patch through the hole while holding the string.

make good with a final smooth coat of general-purpose filler or finish plaster, ensuring the surface is level.

REPAIRING LATH-AND-PLASTER

Holes in lath-and-plaster ceilings and walls can be repaired in the same way as holes in normal plastered surfaces, provided the laths are intact. First brush the laths with PVA (white) adhesive to reduce absorbency, then repair with general-purpose filler, deep-gap filler or repair plaster. If the laths have broken, cut back the plaster until you expose the vertical studs. Cut a piece of plasterboard (gypsum board) to size and nail it in place before filling the hole.

5 Fill the hole with plaster while holding the patch tightly in place with the string.

ABOVE To repair damaged lath and plaster, cut back the old plaster, removing any split wooden laths and square off the edges. Cut a new plasterboard patch to fit the hole and nail it in place. Add support strips if it is a large patch. Complete the repair by plastering over the patch after filling and taping the edges all around.

CONCEALING THE CEILING-TO-WALL JOINT

Coving (crown molding), a quadrant-shaped moulding made from polystyrene, plaster or timber is fitted between the walls and ceiling of a room. It has two functions: to be decorative and to conceal the joint between the walls and ceiling. An ornate coving may be referred to as a cornice; old plaster cornices may be clogged with years of paint and need cleaning to reveal the detail.

PREPARING FOR COVING

Using a short length of coving as a guide, draw pencil lines all around the room, on the wall and ceiling, to indicate the position of the coving. Make sure the lines are straight and continuous. If you are fitting polystyrene or plaster coving, any wall and ceiling coverings must be stripped off between the pencil marks. Run a trimming knife along the lines, then lift the paper with a flat stripping knife, using water and wallpaper stripper if necessary.

If you are fitting plaster coving, score the surfaces of the walls and ceiling with the edge of a filling or putty knife, or trowel, to provide a key for the adhesive.

LEFT Plaster coving is held in place with adhesive (plus nails if heavy) and painted.

LEFT Timber coving is nailed in place and usually varnished or stained (nail holes filled).

LEFT Paper-covered polystyrene coving is held in place with adhesive and it is usually painted.

LEFT Plain polystyrene coving is held in place with adhesive and usually left untreated.

DEALING WITH CORNERS

With polystyrene and plaster coving, you can often buy moulded internal and external corner pieces that fit over the coving at corners, saving you the trouble of having to make neat joints. With timber coving, you may find pre-scribed ends to fit both internal and external corners.

If you have no ready-made corners, you will have to cut 45-degree mitres on the ends of lengths of coving where they meet at a corner. Special jigs or paper templates are often sold with polystyrene and plaster coving to help with this. The alternative is a deep mitre box. For plaster and wood, use a fine-toothed panel or tenon saw to cut the coving; with polystyrene, use a sharp trimming knife. Be prepared to make slight adjustments to the mitres if the room is not absolutely square.

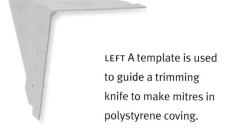

LEFT A template is used to guide a trimming knife to make mitres in polystyrene coving.

PRACTICAL TIP

• When removing wire nails used to hold coving temporarily in place, employ pliers rather than pincers or a claw hammer, which could damage the mouldings.

POLYSTYRENE COVING

The corner pieces for polystyrene coving have square ends designed to be butted against the straight pieces. Start by fitting an internal corner, spreading the recommended adhesive and simply pushing the coving into place. Then fit the straight pieces, working toward the next corner, where you may have to cut a straight piece to fit.

If the walls are uneven, it is better to use ceramic tile adhesive rather than the coving adhesive, since it will provide a thicker adhesive bed.

PLASTER COVING

Special adhesive is available for fixing plaster coving, and it should be spread on the back edges of the mouldings. To hold the coving in place while the adhesive sets, drive wire nails into the wall and ceiling along the edges of the coving (not through the coving), after using a damp cloth to remove excess adhesive that is squeezed out along the joints. Once the adhesive has set, remove the pins and, if necessary, make good the corners and joints with plaster filler (spackle).

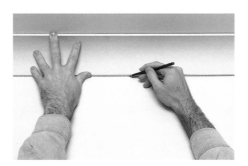

1 Use the coving and mark out two parallel guidelines on the wall and ceiling of the room.

2 Remove old coverings. Score the surface of painted or plaster walls to improve adhesion.

3 Cut the mitre for the corner, press the length into place and support with nails.

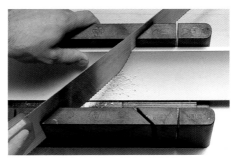

4 Cut a mitre using a mitre box and tenon or panel saw.

5 Butter the back edges of the plaster coving with good adhesive.

6 Fit the adjacent corner piece which has been carefully mitred for an external corner.

TIMBER COVING

This could be put up with adhesive in the same way as plaster coving, but it is easier to use panel pins, making sure they will protrude about 20mm (¾in) from the back of the moulding. Drive them home with a nail punch, then use matching wood filler applied with a putty knife to conceal the holes.

As an alternative to mitring internal corners, they can be scribed – that is, the end of one piece of moulding is cut to the profile of the adjacent piece. The first piece is cut square to butt tightly into the corner, and the second piece fits over it.

External corners will have to be mitred, and all corners must be made good with wood filler once the coving is in place.

7 Complete the external corner with another length of coving, butting the ends together.

8 Fill any gaps at external and internal angles with cellulose filler and sand down once dry.

FIXING TIMBER COVING

1 Fix with a punch and panel pins (brads).

2 Fill the nail holes with matching wood filler.

REPLACING WINDOW GLASS

Replacing broken window glass is a common do-it-yourself job, and something that is worth learning how to do properly. Working with normal window panes is quite straightforward (though care is needed), but replacing the glass in a leaded-light window is trickier. That said, it is well within the scope of anyone with patience and a practical frame of mind.

TYPES OF GLASS

Most window glass used in our homes is 4mm (³⁄₁₆in) float glass, although small panes may be 3mm (⅛in) and large panes may be 6mm (¼in) or more in thickness.

Large panes of glass and glass in vulnerable areas, such as in doors, in panels next to doors or at low level, are likely to be one of two types of safety glass. Toughened glass is heat treated so that it is less likely to break, and when it does it shatters into tiny fragments; laminated glass comprises two thin panes of glass with a plastic layer between them, so

that if the glass breaks, it remains stuck to the plastic interlayer.

In all cases, replace like with like. If in doubt, take a piece of the old glass to your supplier when buying a replacement.

REMOVING THE OLD GLASS

The first step is to remove the old glass immediately, making sure you wear stout gloves that cover your wrists. Collect the glass in newspaper or a cardboard box and dispose of it safely and carefully; your glass supplier may be prepared to accept the broken pieces for recycling. An

PRACTICAL TIP

• When removing broken glass from a window, apply a criss-cross pattern of adhesive tape to the pane to prevent the glass from flying around.

old chisel can be used to chop out all the old putty – do not use a good one, as its blade will be damaged by the sprigs (or clips in a metal frame) that hold the glass in place. Pull out the sprigs or clips and remove all the old putty from the recess.

REPLACING BROKEN GLASS

1 Remove the broken glass, wearing gloves to prevent cuts.

2 Use an old chisel to remove the old putty from the rebate.

3 Pull out the old glazing sprigs with pincers from the frames.

4 Squeeze a thin layer of putty into the corners of the frame.

5 Position the new glass in place with equal clearance all round.

6 Tap in the glazing sprigs at 300mm (12in) intervals.

7 Add more putty and neaten it to a 45-degree bevel.

8 Trim the excess on the inside and outside. Leave to harden.

MEASURING UP

Take measurements of the width and height of the recess in several places. The size of glass you need is 3mm (⅛in) less than the size of the recess. If in doubt, cut a cardboard template to fit and take this with you to the glass supplier. Reckon on buying some new glazing sprigs or clips to hold the glass in place, and buy the correct type of putty – either for timber or for metal windows.

FITTING THE NEW GLASS

Check that the glass fits the recess without binding anywhere, then put it in a safe place.

Take a small amount of putty and work it in your hands until it is pliable; if it sticks to your fingers, roll it out on newspaper to remove some of the oil. When it is workable, begin pressing a layer into the window recess, squeezing it out of the palm of your hand between thumb and forefinger rather like toothpaste.

Put the glass in place, resting it on a couple of matchsticks (wooden matches), and press it gently into the opening until putty is squeezed out at the back – press on the sides of the glass, not the centre. Then fit the glazing sprigs, sliding the head of the hammer along the surface of the glass, or re-fit the clips. Remove putty that has squeezed out on the inside of the window.

Finally, add more putty to the outside of the window, using the same thumb and forefinger technique, until you have a good bead all the way around the glass.

Take a putty knife and smooth off this bead at an angle of 45 degrees, pushing the putty into the edges of the frame as you draw the putty

REPLACING GLASS IN LEAD CAMES

1 Use a sharp trimming knife to cut through the cames at the corners at 45 degrees.

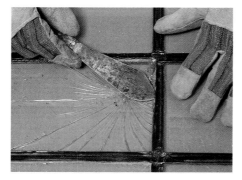

2 Lever up and fold back the cames all round the pane to remove the old glass.

3 With the new glass in place, press the cames back into place with a seam roller.

4 Fuse the lead together at the corners using a small electric soldering iron.

knife along it. Make neat mitres at the corners. If the knife sticks, wet it with water. Leave the putty for about 14 days before painting over it to disguise and seal the joints, allowing the paint to overlap on to the glass to prevent moisture from seeping down into the frame.

REPLACING LEADED LIGHTS

If the glass in a leaded-light window has broken, you will need a really sharp trimming knife to cut through the lead cames at the corners. Make each cut at an angle of 45 degrees so that you can lever up and fold back the edges of the cames securing the broken pane and lift the glass out. Measure the recess exactly and buy a piece of glass of the same thickness

and slightly smaller all round. Put the replacement glass in its recess using a small amount of putty mixed with a little black powder paint.

Fold the lead cames back on to the glass neatly, pressing them down with something like the handle of a spoon or a rounded piece of wood and finishing off with a wallpaper seam roller. Finally, fuse the mitred corners together with a small electric soldering iron and some resin-cored solder.

Many leaded light windows will have one or more panes of coloured glass. The best place to look for authentic replacements for these will be in an architectural salvage yard. A glass merchant can cut a piece of old glass down to size for you.

REPAIRING WINDOWS

The most obvious signs that there is something wrong with a window are when it starts to rattle in the wind or to stick, making it difficult to open and close. Rattling is most likely to be caused by worn hinges or wear of the window itself; sticking by swelling of the wood, build-up of paint or movement of the frame joints. All these faults can be repaired.

REPAIRING HINGES

Loose or worn hinges are often a cause of window problems. To start with, try tightening the screws or replacing them with slightly longer screws of the same gauge. If that does not work, replace the hinges with new ones of the same size and type plus new screws. Remember that steel hinges will rust quickly, so apply suitable primer immediately and then repaint to match the window when this has dried.

Check the opening and closing of the window. If the window is sticking on the far edge, it may be necessary to deepen the recess for one or both hinges; if it binds on the closing edge, one or both recesses will be too deep and may need to be packed out with cardboard. A rattling window can often be cured by fitting draught-excluder strip. Measure the gap, then buy a suitable draught excluder.

ABOVE A loose window joint can be re-glued with fresh adhesive. Clamp it up while the adhesive dries.

WORN WINDOWS

Sash windows are particularly prone to wear. The best answer is to remove the windows and fit brush-pile draught excluder inside the sash channel. A new catch to hold the windows together may also be necessary. Fit a new inner staff bead around the window so that it fits more closely against the inner sash.

WARPED WINDOWS

Timber, hinged windows can sometimes warp, so that they meet the frame only at the top or at the bottom. The best way to cure this is to fit some mortise window locks, which fit into holes cut in the actual window, with the bolts shooting into more holes in the frame. These allow the window to be held in the correct position (get someone to push from the outside while you lock it) so that the warp will self correct. You could position a tiny block of wood between the window and frame so that the warp is over-corrected – do not overdo this or you will break the glass.

PRACTICAL TIP

• When replacing painted steel hinges with brass versions, always use brass screws to match.

DEALING WITH BINDING WINDOWS

ABOVE A binding window may be cured simply by tightening the hinge screws or replacing them with longer ones.

ABOVE If a window is binding on the far side, it may be that the hinge recesses need to be deepened with a chisel.

ABOVE A sticking window may be swollen or have too much paint on it. Plane down the leading edge of the window.

1 To reinforce a glued window joint, drill holes across the joint.

2 Then, hammer in adhesive-covered dowels of the same size.

3 When the adhesive has dried, chisel or plane the dowels flush.

STICKING WINDOWS

Over time, a build-up of paint may cause windows to stick, especially when the weather is damp and the wood begins to swell. Use a plane to cut down the offending areas, which is much easier if you remove the window from its frame, then repaint before refitting the window.

Make sure that all bare wood is covered with paint, as this will prevent water from getting in, which causes the wood to swell. Also, check that the putty is in good condition and doing its job of keeping the water out and the glass in.

LOOSE WINDOW JOINTS

If the paint on a timber window has been allowed to deteriorate, the joints may have dried out and shrunk, causing the window to sag and stick in the frame.

Remove the window and strip off the old paint. You will be able to see the gaps in a loose mortise-and-tenon joint, and it should be possible to work wood glue into these. Use sash clamps to keep the window square while the adhesive dries. There may be wedges in the mortise-and-tenon joint that you can replace with new glued-in wedges as with

doors. If not, you can drill holes across the joint and glue in lengths of dowel to reinforce it. Use a proper dowel drill – 6, 8 or 10mm (¼, ⁵⁄₁₆ or ⅜in) – and fit two dowels per joint. Chisel or plane the dowels flush once the adhesive has dried.

The alternative is to fit an L-shaped reinforcing bracket to each loose window corner. Make sure the window is perfectly square before you fit these and, for neatness, chisel out a recess in the face of the window so that the bracket is flush with the surface, or slightly below so that it can be covered with filler.

1 To fit an L-shaped corner reinforcing bracket, first chisel out a recess.

2 Screw the bracket in place so that it is below the surface.

3 Fill over the bracket and smooth down once the filler has dried.

REPAIRING WINDOW SILLS

A wooden sill is often the first part of a window to need repair, as the rain that falls on the window drips on to the sill and some of it may collect, resulting in flaking paint or crumbling, rotten wood. The treatment ranges from simple repainting to replacement. Since sills project from the wall, they are also prone to impact damage, which can affect concrete and stone sills.

WET ROT

This can be recognized by softening and darkening of the wood and often by severe splintering, the rotten wood falling out. Fortunately, it is fairly easy to repair; on the other hand, dry rot – recognizable by white strands on the surface and a musty smell – requires the services of a professional.

Provided the damage is not so severe that sill replacement is a better option, the first thing to do is remove all the rotten wood with a sharp chisel until you get back to sound, dry wood. Use a hot-air gun if necessary to dry out the wood.

Brush the wood with a wood hardener solution and leave this to dry. This prepares the wood for the application of exterior wood filler. Although this sets hard, it retains sufficient flexibility to be able to move with the wood as it expands and contracts with varying temperatures and humidity. The wood filler can be applied with a filling or putty knife and should be left to set. Substantial damage may need two or even three layers.

Once the filler has hardened, it can be sanded down and the whole area painted to match the surrounding wood – it is probably best to repaint the whole sill.

Some wet-rot repair systems include wood preservative sticks or tablets that you put in drilled holes in the wood surrounding the repair area to prevent future rot. The holes are concealed when the damaged area is filled.

A wet rot system cannot be used to make good dry rot, which can affect masonry as well as woodwork. In this situation, all damaged wood must be completely removed (along with any affected bricks and mortar) and the areas must be professionally sterilized before replacement materials are installed.

REPAIRING WET ROT

1 Chisel out all the rotten wood, making sure only sound wood is left.

2 Brush the sound wood with hardener and leave to dry as recommended.

3 To fit wood preservative sticks, drill holes in the sound wood.

4 Push preservative sticks into the drilled holes and below the surface.

5 Fill the damaged area with exterior wood filler. Leave to dry before sanding.

REPLACING A WOODEN SILL

If only part of a sill needs replacing, you may be able to cut out the damaged section and fashion a replacement, screwing and gluing it in place. However, it is not always easy to achieve a perfect match.

Replacing the whole window sill may be easier than you think, and it can be done without removing the window frame.

First remove any opening windows and take out the glass from the fixed windows. Remove the window board, or inner sill, and saw down through the sill as close as possible to the jambs. Slide out the cut sill sections, then saw through the tenon joints between the jambs and the ends of the sill to remove them. Clean the brickwork below the sill and dry it if necessary.

Cut a new sill to the correct length and, if necessary, cut slots in the ends to fit under the jambs. Prime the sill and the ends of the

jambs and leave to dry. Put the new sill in position on a mortar bed, driving in timber wedges to force it up against the bottom of the jambs before inserting countersunk screws at an angle through the jambs and into the sill. Fill the screw holes before painting.

Glue in wooden blocks to fill any gaps between the jambs and sill, and add more mortar under the window sill if necessary.

1 Cut out the old window sill close to the jambs after removing the inner window board.

2 Put in a new window sill, trimming it to fit underneath the jambs.

3 Secure the new window sill with screws angled down through the jambs.

REPAIRING A CONCRETE OR STONE SILL

A simple crack or small hole in a concrete or stone sill can be repaired in much the same way that you deal with a crack or hole in a wall or ceiling, using an appropriate exterior filler or ready-mixed mortar.

Damage to the edge is more difficult to repair, as it involves building timber shuttering to hold the new concrete while it sets.

Chisel away all loose concrete before fitting the shuttering, using temporary timber supports. Then fill the damaged area with fresh concrete – use dry readymix – using a trowel. Once the concrete has

completely set, you can remove the shuttering. A similar arrangement is used to replace a whole concrete or stone sill, but in this case, it must

take the form of a box with a length of rope pinned along the bottom to provide a former for the window sill's drip groove.

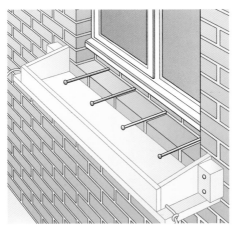

ABOVE Fit shuttering for a new concrete window sill with a drip groove rope.

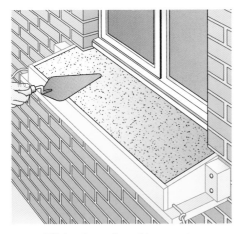

ABOVE Fill the shuttering with concrete, making sure the surface is level.

Rehanging a Door

There may be occasions when the way in which a door opens is not the most convenient. Switching the hinges from one side to the other may provide a more attractive view of the room as the door is opened or allow better use of the wall space. Alternatively, making the door open outward may create more useful space. However, never have a door opening outwards on to a stairway.

Switching the hinged side

When switching the hinged edge of a door from one side to the other, you will need to cut a new mortise for the latch and drill new holes for the door handle spindles. The old latch mortise and spindle holes can be filled by gluing in small blocks of wood and lengths of dowel. Leave the blocks and dowels slightly proud of the surface, then plane and sand them flush when the glue has dried. If you reverse the door, you will be able to use the old latch and door handle spindle holes, but the latch itself will need to be turned around.

You will need to cut a new slot for the striker and striking plate (keeper) on the other side of the frame, and fill the old recess with a thin block of wood stuck in place. Again, make this oversize, planing and sanding it flush once the adhesive has dried.

You will also need to chisel out new recesses for the hinges in both the door and the frame; if the door is reversed, you may be able to use part of the old hinge recesses in the door and need only fill the unused portions. Fill the old hinge recesses with thin blocks of wood glued into place and sanded flush.

If the door has rising butts or other handed hinges, these will need to be replaced.

After rehanging the door, the light switch may be in the wrong place if it is in the room the door opens into. There are two choices here: reposition it on the other side of the door (means running a new wire) or move it across the wall so that it is outside the room, but more or less in the same place (little or no new wire, but possible problems securing the switch mounting box).

Reversing doors

When rehanging a door, it can reduce the amount of work required if you reverse the door – that is, turn it so that the side which faced inwards now faces outwards. This is very true when changing the hinges from left to right or the other way round. There are, however, two problems with doing this. The first is that the two sides of the door may be painted in different colours, which will mean a complete repainting job.

The second is that the door may not fit properly the other way round. Doors and frames can both move slightly over time and while the door will operate perfectly well fitted one way it may bind or catch when fitted the other way.

Filling a recess

1 To fill an old hinge recess, cut a sliver of wood slightly over size.

2 Add adhesive and tap the wood sliver down into the recess.

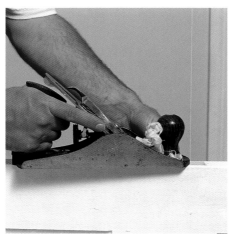

3 When the adhesive has set, plane the surface flush and smooth.

IN TO OUT

When making a door open outward, you will be able to use the same latch and handle positions if the door is hung from the same side of the frame. You will have to reverse the latch, but will be able to make use of parts of the hinge recesses in the door. However, you will need to reposition the striking plate and make new hinge recesses in the frame, as described previously.

The one extra job will be to move the door stop, unless this is positioned centrally in the frame. Moving the door stop needs care to avoid splitting it – slide a chisel in behind the stop and lever it out. Remove the sides before the top, starting in the middle.

When repositioning the door stop, hang the door first, so that you can be sure that the stop fits snugly against the door all round. You can use the same nails to secure it, but reposition them and fill the old holes before repainting.

If you change the side of the frame from which the door is hung (as well as changing it from in to out), you can retain the existing door hinge, latch and door handle positions, although new recesses must still be cut in the frame for the hinges and striking plate, and the old ones filled.

PRACTICAL TIP

• To prevent the paint from chipping when you remove a doorstop, run a trimming knife blade along the joint between doorstop and frame to cut through the paint.

CHANGING DOOR HANDLES

1 Remove the existing door handle and latch from the door, along with the door spindle.

2 Fill the latch recess (not shown) and plug the handle spindle hole with dowel. Fill holes.

3 On the other side of the door, cut a recess for the latch and drill a hole for the spindle.

4 Fit the latch and the door spindle. Now fit the new door handle (here with a keyhole).

REPOSITIONING THE DOOR STOP

1 Slide a chisel under the door stop in order to lever it out.

2 Nail it to the door frame in its new position and fill in any nail holes.

REPAIRING DOORS

Doors can develop all sorts of problems, from simple squeaks and rattles to suddenly refusing to open and shut properly. Fortunately, most of the problems are easy to solve, though for most door repairs you will need to remove the door from the frame. Some faults can be cured by fitting a draught excluder and others by fitting a weatherboard.

SQUEAKS

A door normally squeaks simply because the hinges need oiling. Often you can dribble sufficient oil on to the hinges with the door in place, but if they are caked in dirt and paint, it is best to remove the door and work the hinges back and forth with oil before replacing it.

A door may also squeak if the hinges are binding, usually because the recesses have been cut too deep into the door and/or frame. The solution is simple: unscrew each half of each hinge in turn, place a piece of cardboard behind the hinge and refit the screws. Experiment until the door hangs correctly – you may need more than one thickness of cardboard (or thin plywood).

A door can also bind because the screws are sticking out of the hinge. Normally these can simply be retightened; if they will not hold, fit longer ones of the same gauge, or a smaller size if the original screws had heads that were too large for the countersinks in the hinge.

RATTLES

The simplest way to stop any door rattling is to fit a draught excluder. With an internal door, you could also try moving the door stop; with all types of door, you could try moving the latch striking plate, although this is not easy – drilling out and filling the old screw holes with glued-in dowels helps.

BINDING

External doors often bind during cold, damp weather, becoming free again when the weather is dry and warm. This is a sign that the bottom of the door was not sealed when the door was painted, allowing moisture to get in and swell the door.

Binding doors can also be caused by a build-up of paint on the leading (non-hinge) edge. The cure is to remove the door and then to plane

PRACTICAL TIP

• Door hinge screws are often caked with paint and can be very difficult to turn. Clean the paint out with a sharp screwdriver, held at an angle to the slot and tapped gently with a hammer. To release a stiff screw, place the screwdriver blade in the slot and strike the end of the handle smartly with a hammer, trying, in effect, to push the screw further in. If this does not work, try tightening the screw before unscrewing it.

down the leading edge, repainting it once the door has been fitted. Add at least one coat of primer to the bottom of the door to prevent more moisture from getting in.

If a door binds at the bottom, it may be because the hinges have worked loose. Try tightening the screws, fitting larger or longer screws if necessary. If this does not work and the door joints have not worked loose, you will have to remove the door and plane down the part that is rubbing. Use a block plane, working toward the centre of the door. Then repaint the bottom of the door. With an internal door, you may be able to remove sufficient material by laying a sheet of sandpaper on the floor (abrasive side up) and working the door back and forth across it. A door can bind seriously when you have fitted a new carpet or other

ADJUSTING HINGES

1 Pack a hinge with cardboard to prevent a door binding.

2 Fit longer screws to a hinge if the old ones have lost their grip.

ABOVE Take the door off its hinges and plane the leading edge of a door if it is sticking.

ABOVE Run the base of a door over sandpaper if it is binding.

ABOVE Use a door trimming saw to adjust the height after fitting a new carpet.

floorcovering. In this case, remove the door and cut a strip off the bottom with a circular saw fitted with a rip guide. If there are several doors to shorten, consider hiring a door trimming saw, which can be used with the doors in place.

LOOSE JOINTS

Most doors will have a mortise-and-tenon joint at each corner where the side members, or stiles, meet the top and bottom rails. These can work loose with age.

You do not need to take the door apart: simply remove it, prise out any wedges, cut new wedges and glue them in place. For added security or

if there are no wedges, drill 10mm (⅜in) holes through each stile and the tenon, and glue in 10mm (⅜in) dowels, planing them flush once the adhesive has dried. When repairing a door in this way, use sash clamps first to square it up and then to hold it square while the glue dries.

WARPED DOOR

If a door has become warped, you can straighten it with pairs of clamps, stout lengths of wood and packing blocks. Mount the door between the timbers, say lengths of 50 x 100mm (2 x 4in), and position the packing blocks to force the door in the opposite direction to the warp.

Force it beyond straight by tightening up the clamps and leave for as long as you can. When the clamps are removed, the door should be straight.

FITTING A WEATHERBOARD

A weatherboard is a shaped piece of wood screwed to the bottom of a door to throw rainwater clear. For the best result, drill clearance holes for the screws, then counterbore them with a drill of the same size as the screw heads. That way, the screw heads will be below the surface and can be concealed by gluing in timber plugs.

ABOVE Fit a weatherboard with screws tightened into pre-drilled holes.

ABOVE Reinforce mortise-and-tenon joints with new tapering wedges.

ABOVE Straighten a warped door with timbers, clamps and packing blocks.

Fitting Doors

There is quite a lot to do when fitting a new or replacement door – even if it is the right size. You will need to fit the hinges to the door, together with some form of latch and may need to cut new recesses in the frame for the hinges and striking plate. If the door latch has a lock, you will need to drill and chisel out keyholes.

Size

Doors come in standard sizes, but you may need to trim the sides of a door with a plane or the ends with a saw before fitting it. There needs to be around 3mm (⅛in) clearance at the sides and top, and 5mm (³⁄₁₆in) at the bottom. Always take equal amounts off each side or end, and if planing the top and bottom, work from the edges toward the centre to prevent the wood splitting.

Hinges

A solid hardwood external door will need three substantial hinges: typically 100mm (4in), but most internal doors can be hung on two 75mm (3in) hinges. If you are using brass hinges, always use brass screws.

Choose the hinge positions, using an existing door as a guide – some hollow flush doors incorporate hinge blocks of solid wood – and mark lines across the edge of the door with the aid of a try square. Then use either a hinge or a marking gauge set to the width of the hinge to mark out the recesses – each hinge should end up so that only the knuckle protrudes from the edge of the door. Also mark the thickness on the face of the door.

Cut out the recesses with a mallet and chisel, first cutting down along the lines with the chisel held vertically, then removing the wood with the chisel held at an angle, bevel down to prevent digging in. Take great care not to go beyond the marked recesses. When the hinges fit snugly, make pilot holes for the screws with a small drill or bradawl and screw the hinges in place.

Offer the door up to the frame, propping it on 5mm (³⁄₁₆in) blocks, and transfer the positions of the hinges on to the frame. Cut the recesses in the same way, check the fit, make pilot holes and, with the door propped on the blocks again, secure the hinges to the frame. Check that the door swings freely and closes properly without catching the frame. If necessary, remove the door and deepen the hinge recesses, or pack them out with cardboard.

Fitting hinges

1 Mark out the hinge using the hinge itself as a guide.

2 Cut a recess for the hinge with a chisel and wooden mallet.

3 Clean up the hinge recess, working from the side. Secure the hinge.

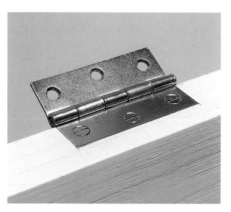

4 The hinge should sit snugly in its recess with the knuckle protruding.

Practical tip

• As a guide for drilling holes to a specific depth, wrap insulating or masking tape around the drill shank at the depth required.

1 Mark out the mortise lock using a mortise gauge.

2 After drilling out the main recess, remove the rest of the wood with a chisel.

3 Cut out a keyhole and spindle hole. Fit the lock and spindle and then the handle.

LATCHES AND LOCKS

Most doors are fitted with a mortise latch, ranging from a simple spring-operated affair to a sturdy high-security lock. The method of fitting is the same, except that with a lock you will need to make keyholes.

Check the instructions and mark out the position of the latch or lock and the handle spindle holes on the door – some hollow flush doors will have a solid block to take the latch/lock. To make the mortise, first drill as many large holes as you can within the outline, then use a chisel to remove the remaining wood. Put the latch/lock in place and mark around the foreplate so that you can chisel out a housing for this – you may also need to deepen the main hole. Drill the handle spindle holes, checking the fit of the latch/lock and the positions of the handles.

Fit the latch/lock to the door and use it to transfer the position of the bolt to the door frame. Draw the outline of the striking plate, double checking its position in relation to the door stop – too close and the latch will not work, too far away and the door will rattle. Drill and chisel out recesses for the plate and screw it in place. Check the latch/lock operation; if necessary, reposition it.

LETTER PLATE

This needs only a large rectangular hole and two smaller holes to fit it. Mark out the position of these on the door – in a solid central rail or bottom rail or, possibly, vertically on the closing stile. Drill the two small holes (for the letter plate securing bolts) and drill largish holes at each corner of the main outline to start the jigsaw (saber saw). Cut along the marked lines, working from the outside of the door, so that any splintering is covered by the letter plate. Do not force the saw or its blade will bend. Clean up the hole with a file and fit the letter plate.

FITTING A LETTER PLATE

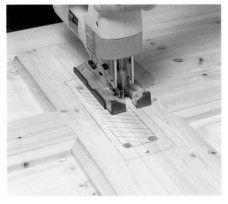

1 Work from the outside of the door. Mark out the letter plate and drill holes for the bolts.

2 Drill holes at the corners of the marked out letter plate and finish cutting with a jigsaw.

3 Fit the letter plate from the outside, securing the nuts inside.

REPAIRING STAIRS

The most common problem with stairs is that they creak. However, they may also suffer from physical damage and from missing parts, especially beneath the treads. The ease with which stairs may be repaired will depend partly on whether you have access to the underside. In some cases, plaster or boards may conceal it, which means working only from above.

HOW STAIRS ARE BUILT

The flat parts of stairs that you walk on are called treads; the vertical sections connecting them are called risers. Treads and risers are joined to one another by various means: butt joints, housing joints or tongued-and-grooved joints. Both treads and risers are joined to the side timbers (strings) by butt joints if the strings are "open", that is shaped to follow the line of the treads and risers, or by housing joints if the strings are "closed", that is having parallel sides. The housing joints in closed strings are reinforced by long, thin glued-in wedges, while in both cases the joint between the front of each tread and the riser below is usually reinforced by small glued-in triangular blocks.

BLOCKS

Reinforcing blocks can work loose, and some may be missing altogether. If blocks are missing, you can make new ones by cutting diagonally down through a piece of 50mm (2in)

REPLACING BLOCKS

1 Clean the old adhesive off loose reinforcing blocks and add fresh adhesive on the two meeting sides.

2 When putting the blocks back into place, screw them to both the tread and the riser to hold them securely.

square timber. When fitting new blocks, or refitting old ones, screw them to both tread and riser as well as applying wood adhesive. With an existing loose block, it may be possible to prise open the joint to squeeze in some adhesive.

WEDGES

Tapered wedges are used to hold the risers and treads firmly in closed strings, but with age, the wedges may become loose. It is best to

remove all loose wedges so that you can clean them and the grooves they fit in of all traces of old glue. If any wedges are missing, make replacements by cutting tapered strips from a piece of timber cut to length, using an old wedge as a guide.

Apply glue to the wedge and its groove, then hammer the vertical wedges home first, followed by the horizontal ones, which should make contact with the vertical wedges at the bottom.

REPLACING WEDGES

1 If any of the tapered wedges are missing, cut fresh ones from a block of wood.

2 Before applying each wedge, coat each side with adhesive. Remove excess afterwards.

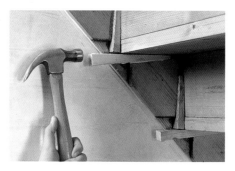

3 Hammer the wedges into place; the horizontal ones under the vertical ones.

SECURING TREADS

1 If you have access from underneath, drive screws up through the backs of treads into the bottom of the risers.

2 If access is denied, cut recesses towards the back of the tread and front of the riser and fit L-shaped brackets to secure the joint.

3 To secure the front of a loose tread, drill holes down exactly into the centre of the riser below and fit screws.

SECURING TREADS

If the joint between the back of a tread and the riser above is loose, you can insert reinforcing screws from below, through the back of the tread into the bottom of the riser. Where access to the underside is impossible, reinforce this joint from above with a couple of L-shaped brackets recessed into the back of the tread and the front of the riser. Make the recesses slightly deeper than the thickness of the brackets and screw them in place.

If the joint between the front of a tread and the riser below is loose, and you cannot get below to reglue the blocks and/or wedges, you can reinforce the joint with screws. Drill pilot holes down through the tread into the riser, making sure they are centred in the riser, and enlarge the holes in the tread to clearance size before driving countersunk screws through the tread into the riser.

If possible, prise the joint apart with a bolster (stonecutter's) chisel, brush out any dirt and squeeze in some glue before screwing the joint together.

REPAIRING A DAMAGED TREAD

It is very unlikely that an entire stair tread will need to be replaced. The more common fault is that part of the nosing, the front curved

PRACTICAL TIP

• When replacing stair treads in an older house, you may well find that the replacement timber you buy will be too small because the original tread was an imperial size (in) and the replacement is metric (mm). If this is the case, buy a larger size and plane it down.

section, will have sustained damage. Fortunately, this can be replaced relatively easily.

Mark out as much of the nosing as you need to remove, drill holes and cut it out using a circular saw, cleaning up the cut with a chisel. Saw the ends to an angle of 45 degrees. Shape a new piece of timber to fit exactly into the space, drilling pilot holes through it and into the existing tread for the securing screws.

Enlarge the holes in the new section and countersink them before gluing and screwing it in place. Drive the screw heads below the surface and screw on a supporting batten (furring strip) while the adhesive dries. Fill the screw holes.

REPAIRING A DAMAGED TREAD

1 Use a circular saw or jigsaw to cut out the damaged section, finishing off the ends of the cut with a sharp chisel.

2 Cut and plane the replacement wood to size and shape before screwing or gluing it in place with a supporting batten.

Repairing Stair Balustrades

"Balustrade" is the name given to the combination of balusters (banisters), posts and handrails that run up the side of a staircase. Over time, these components may become loose or damaged, but repairs are quite straightforward and may range from simply regluing a cracked baluster or repairing a short length of handrail, to replacing the entire assembly.

Baluster repairs

The most likely problem with a balustrade is a cracked or broken baluster. Often, it will be possible to prise a split apart with a wood chisel, squeeze in some adhesive and tape up the split, or clamp it with a small G-clamp, while the adhesive dries. Sometimes, a short dowel glued into a hole drilled across the split will help.

If the baluster is broken, it will be necessary to remove it and either fit a new one or glue together the original piece, which may be your only option if you cannot find a replacement of the same style. You will need to work out how to remove the old baluster. Sometimes, this simply involves pulling out a couple of nails top and bottom. On other occasions, you may need to remove the nosing on the end of a tread, or prise out spacers fitted between the balusters under the handrail and in the base rail, or even cut through the baluster.

You can fashion replacement square balusters yourself and build up broken moulding on a damaged turned baluster with wood filler. If you need to replace a complete turned baluster, you may be able to buy a new one of the same style, if the staircase is not too old, or a second-hand one from an architectural salvage yard, if it is. Failing that, you could approach a local woodturner to make a new one. Otherwise, the broken piece will have to be repaired.

Repairing a handrail

You can buy handrail moulding to repair a broken section, but you need a special type of bolt to hold the sections together. This passes through holes drilled into the ends

Replacing a balustrade

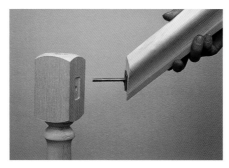

1 If you have an old-fashioned balustrade like this, you may want to replace it completely.

2 Remove the old handrail and the wrought iron sections and prise up the base rail.

3 Cut through all newel posts with a panel saw, keeping the cut square to the post.

7 Hammer the newel post into place, using a piece of scrap wood to protect the top.

8 Cut the handrail to the correct length and angle before joining it to the newel post.

9 Fit a nut to the bracket bolt and tighten it with a socket spanner. Fit the cover plug.

of the new and old handrails, both cut square, and requires "pockets" to be cut out to accommodate the nuts of the bolt. Two additional holes need to be drilled for dowels that prevent the handrail from turning around the bolt. To position these correctly, drill the holes in one part, using a dowelling bit, and fit centre-points into the holes so that their positions can be transferred to the other part.

REPLACING A BALUSTRADE

You can buy kits for replacing a complete balustrade, using the bottom portions of the existing newel posts. The first step is to remove the existing balustrade – handrail, balusters and the bottom rail. Cut through the old newel posts with a panel saw close to the base,

making sure the cuts are square. Then drill a large hole in each stump of newel post to take the end of the new newel post and shape the stump to a gentle curve. The new newel post is glued into place with a dowel to tighten it. The new handrail must be cut to length with the correct angle at each end and secured with the brackets supplied.

The base rail must also be cut to the correct length and angles. Then each baluster can be cut to length, again with the ends at the correct angle, and slotted into the base rail and the underside of the handrail. The balusters are held in place with wooden spacers nailed to the base rail and the underside of the handrail. Special accessories are available to accommodate staircases that have 90-degree turns or half-landings.

PRACTICAL TIPS

• To reinforce a straight break in a baluster, first drill a 10mm (⅜in) hole in the centre of one of the sound sections. Then make a right-angled cut through the baluster, using the thinnest saw blade you can find, such as a junior hacksaw, to remove a portion of the drilled baluster. Glue this to the other broken piece and leave for the adhesive to set. Continue the hole through the glued joint into sound timber. Finally, glue the whole baluster together with a 10mm (⅜in) dowel bridging the original break and the new saw cut.

• When buying a handrail, look for the type that has a grooved underside to hold the balusters firmly and in a straight line.

4 Mark out the hole for the new newel post, drill several holes and lever out the waste.

5 Use a plane (or a planer-file) to give the stump of the newel post a rounded top.

6 Using the dowel supplied, apply adhesive to the newel post and insert it into the hole.

10 Each baluster will have to be cut to the correct angle. Use a sliding bevel to mark it.

11 Spacers fitted to the handrail and to the bottom rail correctly space the balusters.

12 Enhance the final result by sanding and applying a stained varnish to the staircase.

CLEARING SINKS AND DRAINS

The waste pipes leading from sinks, basins, baths and showers can become blocked with all sorts of things – hair, food scraps, grease and so on – so that water will no longer drain freely. There are many tools with which to clean them. Larger soil pipes, to which waste pipes may be connected, and the soil pipes leading from toilets can also become blocked and need bigger versions of the same tools.

PLUNGING

A rubber basin plunger, a rubber cup on the end of a long handle, is used to clear blocked waste pipes by using water pressure.

With the basin, sink, or similar, full and the overflow blocked with a damp cloth, hold the plunger over the waste outlet and pump it up and down. This will force water down the waste pipe and should clear the blockage. A force pump and an aerosol clearer work on the same principle, but create more pressure and can be used with the sink empty.

SINK AUGER

A sink auger, or plumber's snake, is a flexible steel cable with a specially shaped head at one end and sometimes a turning handle at the other. It is passed down through the waste outlet and along the waste pipe until it reaches the blockage, where the head is turned to dislodge the blockage and allow water to flow freely. It cannot be used with a bottle-type trap.

REMOVING THE TRAP

If plunging or using a sink auger does not work, or if the trap is of the bottle type, you will have to remove the trap itself. Place a bucket beneath it and simply unscrew the connections by hand.

If the blockage is in the trap, you should be able to clear it out, dismantling the trap if necessary. If it is farther down the waste pipe, removing the trap will give you a clearer run with a sink auger. Refit the trap, making sure that it is tight.

BLOCKED TOILETS

You can obtain larger versions of sink plungers and force pumps to use in toilets, and also a larger auger. The business end of the auger should be passed round the U-bend until you reach the blockage, when rotating the auger should clear it.

PRACTICAL TIP

• You can help to keep waste pipes, particularly sink wastes, clear by occasionally pouring some washing soda down the waste outlet. This will help to prevent grease from building up.

Chemical clearers can be used in the same way, but are not ideal for total blockages.

ABOVE Blocked waste outlets can be cleared with a sink plunger or a force pump (as here).

ABOVE Use a sink auger, pushed down until it meets the blockage.

ABOVE Unscrew a bottle-type waste trap from a basin to check for blockages.

ABOVE Use rubber gloves and a large plunger to clear a blocked toilet.

ABOVE Use drain rods in an inspection chamber to remove a blockage.

ABOVE Use an auger in a waste gully to clear a blocked drain.

DRAIN ROD HEADS

Plunger

Cleaning wheel

Wormscrew

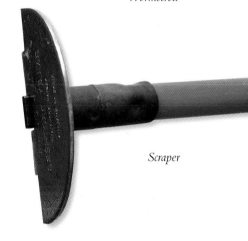

Scraper

Blocked drains and soil pipes

A large auger can also be used to clear blocked underground drains. It should be passed down through an open gully and along the drain until you reach the blockage.

The main soil pipe will run vertically either inside or outside the house. If it is blocked, your best chance of clearing it will be to unscrew an inspection hatch and then either to use an auger or drain rods to dislodge the blockage.

Using drain rods

These are used for clearing drains when there is a blockage between one (full) inspection chamber and the next (empty) one. When you discover the empty chamber, go back to the last full one and rod from there. Drain rod sets come with a choice of heads – plungers to push the blockage along the pipe, scrapers to pull it back and wormscrews or cleaning wheels to dislodge it.

Start with a wormscrew connected to two rods, lowering it to the bottom of the chamber. Feel for the half-round channel at the bottom of the chamber and push the wormscrew along this until it enters the drain at the end. Push it along the drain, add more rods to the free end and only turn the rods clockwise, otherwise they may become unscrewed. Keep working at the obstruction until water flows into the empty chamber, then use the scraper and plunger to clear the underground drain section.

Inspecting a soil pipe

1 To clear a blocked soil pipe, start by unscrewing an inspection hatch.

2 Then remove the inner cover – make sure you are standing well out of the way!

3 Use an auger or drain rod to clear the soil pipe before replacing the cover.

CLEARING AND REPAIRING GUTTERS

The gutters and downpipes of your home are essential to remove rainwater. Nevertheless, they are exposed to the elements and are likely to become blocked, so regular maintenance is necessary to keep them clear and also to keep them in good condition. If you are replacing sections of plastic guttering, make sure you always use the same brand.

CLEARING GUTTERS AND DOWNPIPES

Autumn is the ideal time to clear out gutters, removing leaves, birds' nests and general dirt and debris so that the winter rains can drain away freely. Use a garden trowel or gutter clearing tool to scoop out blockages from the gutters into a bucket, which should be secured to your ladder.

If there is a blockage near to the top of a downpipe, use something like a bent metal coat hanger to pull it out. Blockages farther down can be removed by using drain rods fitted with a wormscrew head.

MAINTENANCE FOR CAST-IRON GUTTERS AND DOWNPIPES

Traditional cast-iron gutters may look very nice, but they can give no end of trouble.

To start with, they rust, so need regular painting to keep them looking good. A more serious

CLEANING OUT GUTTERS

ABOVE You can use a household garden trowel to clean out gutters.

ABOVE Alternatively, use gutter clearing tools specially designed for the job.

problem, however, is that the putty used to seal the joints can dry out, causing leaks.

You may be able to overcome minor joint leaks by cleaning the gutter out and brushing the inside with bituminous paint, but a proper repair will mean unscrewing the joint and replacing the old putty with non-setting mastic (caulking).

Use a hacksaw to cut through the securing bolt if it has rusted in place. Then remove the screws holding the gutter to the fascia board and lift it clear. It will be very heavy – do not drop it, as it will shatter as well as possibly causing damage. Clean the joint faces, apply the mastic and replace the gutter, using a new nut and bolt to connect the sections.

REPAIRING CAST-IRON GUTTERS

ABOVE Prior to painting a cast-iron gutter, clear it out using a wire brush.

ABOVE Treat cast-iron guttering with black bituminous paint to seal leaks.

ABOVE Remove a cast-iron gutter bolt with a hacksaw if it is rusted in place.

DOWNPIPES

A wire balloon fitted into the top of a downpipe will prevent birds from nesting and keep leaves and other debris out. If your downpipe does get blocked, clear with drain rods fitted with a wormscrew.

A crack or hole in a cast-iron gutter can be repaired with a glass fibre repair kit sold for use on car bodywork. Apply the glass fibre sheets over the damage and fill to the level of the surrounding metal with the resin filler provided with the kit. Glass fibre bandage can also be used in the same way for repairing cast-iron downpipes.

MAINTENANCE FOR PLASTIC GUTTERS AND DOWNPIPES

Plastic guttering has largely replaced cast iron and is easier to repair. It is also much easier to replace.

Leaks at the joints between lengths of plastic gutter are prevented by rubber seals, and if these fail it is usually quite easy to replace them. Take the old seal to the shop as a guide when buying a replacement. Otherwise, try cleaning them with some liquid soap to make them more efficient. If an end stop is leaking, replace the rubber seal in this in the same way.

The alternative is to use a gutter repair sealant, available in a cartridge for use with a caulking gun, forcing this into the joint to make a seal. Self-adhesive gutter repair tape is also available for sealing splits in plastic gutters and covering small holes in gutters and downpipes.

When separating and reconnecting lengths of plastic guttering, note that some types simply snap into their securing brackets, while others have notches cut near the gutter ends to take the clips.

REPAIRING GUTTER BRACKETS

If a gutter is sagging, the most likely cause is failure of the screws that hold a bracket in place. First, remove the section of gutter above the offending bracket.

If the screws have worked loose, it may be possible to retighten them, perhaps replacing them with longer or larger screws; if the holes have become too large, move the bracket slightly to one side, making new holes in the fascia board for the bracket screws. A rise-and-fall bracket is adjustable in height and so allows correction of sagging gutters without the need to remove them.

ABOVE Wearing gloves, use glass fibre to repair a crack in a cast-iron gutter. Remove the gutter from the brackets to make it easier.

REPAIRING PLASTIC GUTTERS

ABOVE Rubber seals in the end stop of plastic guttering can be replaced if they fail.

ABOVE Gutter repair sealant can be used to fix a leaking joint between gutters.

ABOVE Repair a crack in a gutter with gutter repair tape applied to the inside.

REPAIRING PITCHED ROOFS

A pitched house roof may be covered with traditional slates, clay tiles or interlocking concrete tiles. All can fail and work loose; you can repair small areas of damage yourself, but large-scale repairs may mean wholesale replacement of the roof covering, which should be entrusted to a professional roof contractor. Never walk directly on a roof covering; use a proper ladder.

SLATES

The most common cause of roof slates slipping is "nail sickness", that is one or both of the nails holding a slate rusting through. The slate itself may be undamaged and still be on the roof somewhere.

If only one nail has failed, use a slate ripper to cut through the other one. This tool is slid under the slate, hooked around the nail and given a sharp tug to break the nail.

With the slate removed, you will be able to see, between the two exposed slates, one of the timber battens (furring strips) to which the slates are attached. Cut a strip of zinc or lead, about 150 x 25mm (6 x 1in), and nail one end to the exposed batten so that the strip runs down the roof.

Slide the slate back into its original position and secure it by bending the end of the zinc or lead

Slate ripper

Slater's axe (for cutting slates)

strip over the bottom edge. Note that slates at the edges of the roof have mortar fillets beneath them to prevent the wind from blowing debris into the roof space.

REPLACING SLATES

1 Use a slate ripper to cut through a slate nail that is still holding the slate.

2 Slide out the damaged slate, taking care not to let it fall to the ground.

REPLACING A DISLODGED TILE

Most concrete and many clay tiles are held in place by hooks, or nibs, on the top edge, which fit over the roof battens. If these are still intact, a dislodged tile can simply be replaced by gently lifting the surrounding tiles, supporting them on wooden wedges and slipping the tile back into position. If the nibs have broken off, the tile can be replaced in the same way as a slate. Edge tiles also have a fillet of mortar beneath them.

3 Fit a lead or zinc strip by nailing it to the batten (furring strip) under the slate.

4 Slide the old (or replacement) slate into place over the lead or zinc strip.

5 Bend the end of the lead strip over the bottom edge of the slate.

1 Remove loose ridge tiles, clean away debris and apply a fresh bed of mortar.

2 Put the old (or replacement) ridge tile in position, pushing it down into the mortar.

3 With the ridge tile firmly in place, smooth all joints and remove excess mortar.

RIDGE TILES

The curved tiles that run along the top of a tile or slate roof are mortared into place. With age and weathering, one or two may have become loose.

To replace ridge tiles, you need a roof ladder with hooks that fit over the ridge and wheels that allow you to run it up the roof from the top of a conventional ladder. This will provide a safe means of access.

Once you have reached the ridge, remove the loose tiles, then use a small trowel to scrape away crumbling mortar until you reach sound mortar. Dampen the tiles and trowel on a bed of fresh mortar.

Place each ridge tile gently into position, tapping it down with the handle of the trowel. Add mortar to the ends of each ridge tile to fill the joints with its neighbours and scrape off all excess mortar.

VALLEYS

If you have a dual-pitch roof – different parts of the roof pointing in different directions – there will be a lead-lined valley between them to allow rainwater to escape and provide a junction between the tiles. Cracks can occur in the lead, allowing water to leak through.

A severely damaged roof valley will need to be replaced completely – a job for professionals. But simple cracks can be repaired with self-adhesive flashing tape. Once the area around the crack has been cleaned, the tape is applied – sometimes, a primer is needed first – and rolled out flat using something like a wallpaper seam roller.

PRACTICAL TIP

• For securing loose ridge tiles and packing under edge tiles and slates, use a weak mortar mix – no more than three parts sand plus plasticizer to allow some movement and prevent cracking.

1 Clear out any leaves and debris from a leaking roof valley using a stiff brush.

2 Roll out self-adhesive flashing tape to repair the roof valley.

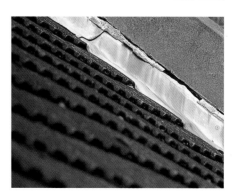

ABOVE Lead flashing is used to seal between a pitched roof and a parapet wall.

Repairing Flat Roofs

Unless expensive materials have been used, the average life of a felted flat roof is about ten to 15 years. If a felted flat roof fails, it is not worth trying to repair it and you should re-cover it. However, there are things you can do to repair minor faults and to extend its life before it needs to be replaced. Failure to act can result in water leaking through to the timbers below and causing rot.

Repairing cracks and blisters

You will need bituminous mastic (caulking) to repair a crack or blister in a felted flat roof. Although quite messy, the job is straightforward.

First remove any loose chippings from around the damaged area with a brush. Using a hot-air gun, soften the felt first if necessary, and brush or scrape away dirt, moss and any other debris. With a crack or split in the roofing felt, pull back the edges; with a blister, make a cross-shaped pattern of cuts in the centre of the blister and peel back the four sections. If any seams are lifting, clean the area below them.

When the underlying surface has dried out – use a hot-air gun to speed this up if necessary – apply mastic to the exposed area and press down the edges of the crack, blister or lifted seam, using something like a wallpaper seam roller. If a crack cannot be closed up, use polyester reinforcing tape or flashing tape to strengthen the repair.

Some emergency roof repair compounds can be used to seal a leaking roof even if it is wet or under water. Instant repair aerosols can be used on damp roofs (and also on leaking flashing or guttering); check the manufacturer's instructions.

If a felted flat roof has several cracks and blisters, or is generally in bad condition, it is possible to waterproof it with either a bituminous emulsion or a longer-lasting elastomeric liquid rubber.

ABOVE A solar-reflective roof seal absorbs less heat, so stays more flexible and will not blister.

Patching a blister

1 Brush all solar-reflective chippings and dirt and debris away from the area to be repaired.

2 If necessary, use a hot air gun to soften the damaged roofing felt before scraping it away.

3 If the roofing felt has blistered, use a trimming knife to cut a cross shape.

4 Apply the repair mastic and work it into the cross and under the felt.

5 Flashing tape can be rolled out to cover up a crack that will not close up.

Re-covering a felted roof

1 Sweep the whole roof clear and treat the surface with fungicide.

2 Apply liquid rubber compound over the entire roof surface.

3 Clean up splashes and recover the roof with loose stone chippings.

The whole roof should be swept clean before treating the surface with fungicide to kill any mould. Carry out any local repairs, then cover the surface with the emulsion or liquid rubber, tipping it out from the container and spreading it with a soft brush or broom. Sponge away any splashes with solvent.

Some bituminous emulsions need a priming coat before the main coat; all liquid rubber compounds are one-coat treatments and they last longer because they remain flexible.

When the emulsion or liquid rubber coating has dried, reapply stone chippings. Use new chippings if the old ones are dirty or have lost their shine – the purpose of stone chippings on flat roofs is to keep them cool by reflecting sunlight.

Roof junctions

The junction between a flat roof and the house wall is particularly prone to damage, allowing water to seep through. The correct way to seal this joint is with lead flashing, inserted into one of the mortar courses of the wall.

If a mortar fillet has been used to seal the junction, or if lead flashing has split, the simplest way to effect a repair is by using a self-adhesive bituminous flashing tape. Choose the appropriate type of tape to the task in hand.

Clean the surfaces that are to be covered and apply any necessary primer before removing the backing paper and pressing down the flashing tape, first with your fingers, then a seam roller. Wear heavy gloves when doing this as it can be messy. The tape can be cut with scissors if required. Make good the mortar joints where any lead flashing meets the house wall, using fresh mortar.

Repairing junctions

1 Use flashing tape to seal porous felt or metal flashings. Brush on a coat of primer.

2 Unroll the flashing tape, peel off the release paper and press the strip into position.

3 Run a seam roller firmly along both edges of the strip to ensure the tape bonds well.

Refelting Flat and Pitched Roofs

If the damage to a felted roof is too serious to repair, refelting is the solution, provided the underlying structure is in good condition. Simple pitched roofs, such as those found on garden sheds, are the simplest; replacing a high-performance flat roof on a house extension or lean-to garage is likely to be much more difficult, though not impossible.

Pitched roofs

In general, a shed roof has only a single layer of felt, but with a fairly generous overlap between sheets to keep rain out. The first step is to rip off all the old felt and remove all the nails. Replace or repair the timber roof decking if necessary and check that the edging timbers are sound. Treat all timber with preservative.

New pieces of felt should be cut, making them 150–200mm (6–8in) longer than the shed roof. Lay the first strip along the bottom of one side of the roof, smoothing any creases with a length of wood. Make sure the ends overlap the ends of the roof evenly and that the bottom edge overlaps the edge of the roof sufficiently to be turned down and project just beyond the eaves. This allows rainwater to drip clear.

Using 13mm (½in) roofing nails, secure the top of the felt strip to the roof, the bottom to the eaves board and the ends to the fascias, folding the corners neatly, and repeat for the other side of the shed. Trim excess felt from the ends of the roof. If the shed is large, lay a second strip on each side nailed at the top, but with the bottom overlapping the first sheet by at least 75mm (3in) and secured by felt adhesive. Fix it at the ends with nails. The final strip is laid over the ridge; cut it to width as well as length so that it overlaps the sheets on the sides of the roof by no more than 75mm (3in). Secure this with adhesive, but nail the ends.

Fit the fascia boards to cover the nailed edges at the ends of the roof.

Refelting a shed roof

1 Cut the felt longer than the roof and unroll the first strip along the bottom of one side.

2 Making sure it overlaps at each end and at the bottom, hammer nails along the top edge.

3 Apply a generous layer of felt adhesive along the top edge of the first strip of felt.

4 Apply the second strip of felt overlapping the first so that the nail heads are covered.

5 Make neat folds at the ends of the roof and nail the felt to the roof boards to secure it.

6 Make the corners waterproof with more felt adhesive. Nail the fascia boards at either end.

RE-COVERING A FELTED FLAT ROOF

Most flat roofs have two or three layers of felt, which will be a more durable type than that used on shed roofs. The top sheet will be capping felt, held down with adhesive.

The first step is to strip off all the existing felt down to bare timber and remove any guttering and flashing. When removing the old felt, notice how it is folded and cut at all corners and edges – make sketches that you can follow later. Check the condition of the roof timber, repairing or replacing it as necessary. Remove all nails and sweep the roof clean.

Most flat roofs have a raised angled lip along two sides to direct rainwater to the third open side, where it flows into a gutter. The fourth side meets the house wall.

Strips for the first layer of felt should be cut to slightly longer than the roof and nailed into place, working toward the gutter, using 18mm (¾in) clout nails. Allow an overlap of at least 50mm (2in) between strips. Make cuts so you can take the felt up and over the angled lips at the edges and up the angled fillet at the house wall, following the sketches you made earlier. Trim the felt flush at the eaves.

Cut a flashing strip about 150mm (6in) wide from the capping felt and lay this along the house wall so that it laps on to the roof. Tuck it into the lowest available mortar joint, having cut out some of the mortar first. If you are adding a second layer, stick it down to the first, using a continuous coat of felt adhesive. Cut the first strip to a different width so that the joints do not coincide with those of the first layer. Lay the first strip on the roof, roll it back half-way to apply adhesive underneath, then repeat the process for the other end. Carry on in this manner for the remaining strips, overlapping them by at least 50mm (2in) and applying felt adhesive along the overlap. Do not take the second layer over the the raised lips. The top layer should be stuck down in the same way as the second, but the detailing at the corners and edges will be different.

Finish off by laying a second flashing strip along the house wall, fixing it into a higher wall mortar joint with fresh mortar, and a folded "apron" along each lipped edge.

BELOW A cross section of a flat roof, showing how it is constructed.

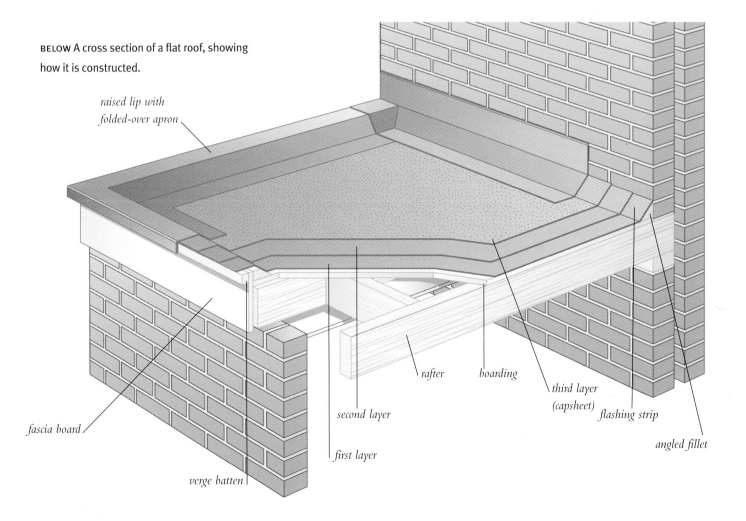

raised lip with folded-over apron

rafter

boarding

third layer (capsheet)

flashing strip

angled fillet

second layer

first layer

verge batten

fascia board

Repairing Fence Posts and Gates

Fences around your home serve the useful purpose of keeping children and pets in and intruders out, as well as providing privacy. However, since most fences are made of wood, they are likely to decay and need attention. There are many ways of overcoming rotting fences. Gates also suffer and must be maintained in good condition, otherwise the security your fence provides will be compromised.

Repairing fence posts

A fence relies on its posts to provide much of its strength and to keep it upright – but because the posts are set in the ground and can get wet, they are prone to rotting, leading to fence collapse.

The most vulnerable part of a fence post is the portion underground. Either this will be completely rotten, making the post unstable, or the post will have snapped off at ground level. In both cases, there are ways to effect a repair using the remaining sound piece of post.

If the fence post is still standing or is attached to a closeboard fence – overlapping vertical boards nailed to triangular-section horizontal (arris) rails – the best way to repair it is with a fence-post spur. This is a short concrete post that you set into the ground next to the broken post. Then you bolt the two together. Start by digging a hole roughly 30cm (1ft) square and 50cm (20in) deep in front of the broken post, that is on your side of the fence; you may need a long cold chisel and a club (spalling) hammer if you encounter concrete.

Place the spur in the hole so that it lines up with the post, then insert coach bolts in the holes in the spur, giving them a tap with a hammer to transfer their positions to the post. Drill holes in the post to take the bolts. Secure the spur to the fence post with the coach bolts and fill the hole around it, first with a layer of

Fitting a fence spur

1 With the fence still standing, dig a large hole – around 30cm (1ft) square – next to the damaged post.

2 Place the fence-post spur in the hole in order to mark the coach bolt holes on the post ready for drilling.

3 Drill holes in the timber post, insert the coach bolts from the other side and secure the spur.

4 Fill the large hole first with hardcore (rubble) and then with concrete. Smooth down the surface and leave to set completely.

hardcore (rubble), then with concrete. If necessary, prop the main post upright while the concrete sets.

With a panel fence, release the adjacent panels from the post and saw through it at ground level. Then hammer a repair spike – a shorter version of the normal fence-post spike – over the rotten wood in the ground. Fit the sound portion of the

post into the socket of the spike and replace the fence panels.

Repairing timber gates

If a timber gate is sagging and dragging on the ground, check first that the posts are upright, using a level and paying particular attention to the hinged side. If a post has rotted, replace it with a new one.

FITTING A REPAIR SPIKE

1 With the fence panels removed, saw through the damaged post at ground level.

2 Using the tool provided, hammer in the repair spike over the rotten post.

3 Fit a new post (or the old post) into the spike and secure it in place.

If it is leaning slightly, it may be possible to force it back, with the gate removed, and ram some hardcore or more concrete into the ground to hold it in place.

Timber gates may also sag if the joints have become loose. You can fit a variety of metal brackets to support the framework of a timber gate: flat L-shaped or T-shaped brackets at the corners where the vertical stiles meet the cross-rails or the diagonal brace, a right-angled bracket on the inside of the frame between stile and cross-rail, and straight flat brackets to repair simple splits. All will look better if they are recessed into the timber so they are flush with the surface. You could alternatively try replacing the main diagonal support brace or fitting longer hinges.

REPAIRING METAL GATES

First, check that the posts are vertical, then that you can move the adjusting nuts — often these will be rusted or clogged with paint. If this is the case, wire brush off the worst of the rust and paint and apply a silicone spray or penetrating oil until you can turn the nuts freely. Finally, adjust the hinges so that the gate no longer rubs on the ground and swings freely but closes properly.

ABOVE Four different types of post spike. From the left: a normal post spike for new posts; a repair spike for rotten posts; a spike for mounting in fresh concrete; a spike for bolting down to a hard surface.

POST LEVELS

A post level can be strapped to a post to ensure it is vertical in both directions.

REPAIRING A SAGGING GATE

ABOVE Fit a replacement diagonal brace to support a timber gate.

ABOVE Using longer hinges is one way to secure a sagging timber gate.

Repairing Fences and Walls

Timber fences are constantly exposed to the effects of rain, sun and wind. Sooner or later, parts of a fence will rot, split, break or simply fall off. Regular treatment with preservative or stain will prolong the life of a fence, but when repairs are necessary, do not delay, otherwise the fence will no longer do its job. Even masonry walls are not immune to the effects of weathering.

Closeboard fences

A closeboard fence consists of two or three horizontal triangular (arris) rails fitted between posts and supporting overlapping vertical lengths of tapered (feather-edge) boarding (pales). The result is an extremely durable and strong fence. Even so, arris rails can split and sag, while individual pales can become damaged. A horizontal gravel board will run along the bottom of the fence to protect the end grain of the vertical pales from ground moisture. Normally, this is easy to replace, as it is held with just a couple of nails or screws.

Usually, a single broken pale can be levered off with a claw hammer and the nails securing it prised out. If they will not budge, hammer them into the arris rail with a nail punch. Cut the replacement pale to the same length and slide its thin edge under the thick edge of the adjacent pale, having levered this clear of the arris rails slightly and removed the nails from it. Then nail through both pales – each nail holds two pales. If you are replacing several pales, use a short piece of wood as a gauge to ensure even overlapping of the pales.

Repairing closeboard fencing

1 Use an old chisel to lever out the damaged pale of a closeboard fence.

2 Slide the replacement pale into place and nail it to the horizontal arris rail.

3 Reinforce a broken arris rail by nailing on a galvanized repair bracket.

4 A flanged galvanized repair bracket will support the broken end of an arris rail.

Repairing arris rails

If an arris rail has split in the middle, you can buy a galvanized repair bracket that simply fits over the rail and is screwed or nailed in place. If necessary, have a helper lever the fence up, using a crowbar (wrecking bar) over a block of wood, while you fit the repair bracket.

A similar repair bracket, but with a flanged end, is available for reconnecting an arris rail that has broken where it is fixed to the fence post. This is screwed or nailed to both the rail and the post. You can use two of these brackets to replace a complete length of arris rail after sawing through the old rail at the ends and levering it from the fence.

Replacing fence panels

A panel fence has posts regularly spaced at 1.83m (6ft) intervals. The panels come in a variety of designs – interwoven, overlapping and imitation closeboard are the most popular – but are all fixed between the posts in the same way, with either clips or nails holding the panels to the posts.

If clips have been used, replacing a broken panel with a new one will be easy, since screws often secure the panel to the clips. If the panel has been nailed in place, you may destroy it as you lever it out.

The new fence panel should fit exactly between the posts and can be secured in the same way. If the new panel is a tight fit at any point, use a planer-file or rasp to trim it; if it is loose, trim a section of the timber from the old panel to fill the gap.

Repairing garden walls

A common problem with garden walls is that bricks suffer from spalling, that is the surface breaks up. This results from water getting into the brick and expanding as it freezes.

Depending on how well the wall has been built, it may be possible to remove the damaged brick and turn it around, using a masonry drill and a thin-bladed plugging chisel to remove the mortar from the joints. However, it is likely that mortar on the back of the brick will prevent its removal. Therefore, the only solution will be to break it up with a bolster

and club hammer, then insert a new brick. Remove all old mortar from the hole, then lay a bed of fresh mortar on the bottom of the hole. Add mortar to the top and sides of the new brick and push it into place, forcing more mortar into gaps, before finishing off the joints to the same profile as the remainder of the wall.

A garden wall can crack along mortar lines, and this often shows a problem with the foundations. There is little alternative to demolishing at least the split section, investigating the problem and making good the foundations before rebuilding it.

Replacing a fence panel

1 To remove a fencing panel, start by levering out the nails holding it in place.

2 You may need to use something like a crowbar in order to lever out the panel.

3 If using clips, nail these in place before sliding the panel through them.

4 Nails are driven through the end section of the panel right into the supporting post.

Removing a damaged brick

1 Remove the mortar around the old brick.

2 Insert a new mortared brick.

3 Repoint the mortar around the replaced brick to the correct profile.

Repairing Steps and Repointing Brickwork

Solid concrete steps are very prone to damage, especially at the edges, while the mortar in brickwork all around the garden is likely to need replacing at some point, or at least freshening up. You need only a minimum of tools to carry out the necessary work, but make sure you have the right safety wear (gloves and safety shoes) and do not work in very cold weather.

Damaged steps

Minor damage in a concrete step, such as small cracks and holes, can be repaired in much the same way as repairing cracks and holes in plaster walls, except that you use an exterior-grade filler, quick-setting cement or mortar made from three parts fine sharp sand to one part cement. Brushing the damaged area with PVA adhesive (white glue) will help the repair compound to

stick. Smooth off the surface of the repair compound with a trowel before it has finally set, as you will not be able to rub it down afterwards. Any repair involving a broken corner or edge, however, will require shuttering to contain the repair compound while it sets.

For small repairs to the edge of a step, you need only a block of wood propped in place; more extensive repairs need complete shuttering.

Exterior-grade plywood is the best material for this. Use three pieces to make a three-sided mould of the correct height. Secure them at the back with timber anchor blocks screwed into wall plugs inserted in the wall alongside the step. For freestanding garden steps, use sash clamps to hold the shuttering.

Before fitting the shuttering, use a wire brush to remove any loose concrete and plant matter from the step. Hack off any split pieces of concrete and then brush the surface with PVA adhesive.

With the shuttering in place, trowel in the repair compound and smooth it off, using the top of the shuttering as a guide. As it begins to dry, when moisture has disappeared from the surface, roughen the surface with a stiff broom or hand brush, then use a small pointing trowel to round off the edges where they meet the shuttering. Remove the shuttering when the filler, cement or mortar has set.

Repairing a concrete step

1 Use a wire brush to remove loose and damaged concrete around the step.

2 Apply a coat of PVA adhesive to the surface to help the repair compound stick.

3 Fit a piece of wood shuttering to the step edge and prop this in place.

4 Using a trowel, fill in the step edge with repair concrete and smooth it out.

5 Remove the shuttering and if necessary, smooth out the surface of the concrete.

BRICKWORK

Failed mortar joints between bricks are not only unsightly, but they also allow water into the wall, damaging the bricks when it freezes. The solution is to repoint the joints with fresh mortar.

First, use a thin-bladed plugging chisel to remove all loose mortar until you reach sound material. Brush all dust from the joints and dampen them with a paintbrush dipped in water or a hand-held garden sprayer.

Use a pointing trowel – a smaller version of a bricklaying trowel – to push fresh mortar into the joints, working on the verticals first, then the horizontals. Carry the mortar to the wall on a hawk – a flat metal plate or wooden board on a handle – then hold this against the wall directly beneath the joint you want to fill. Use the pointing trowel to slice off a thin strip of mortar and press it into the joint.

When you have used one batch of mortar, go back over all the joints, shaping the surface of the mortar to the required profile:

- Weatherstruck – using the edge of the pointing trowel to create a sloping profile that sheds rainwater from the wall. Start with the vertical joints and slope them all in the same direction.
- Recessed – using a square-shaped stick, or special tool.
- Flush – using sacking to rub the surface and expose the sand aggregate in the mortar.
- Concave (or rubbed) – using a rounded stick or a piece of hosepipe and run along the joints to make the profile.

A weatherstruck profile is often used on house walls for its rain-shedding properties, while recessed joints are only appropriate to wall surfaces inside. A concave profile is a good choice for garden walls.

PRACTICAL TIPS

- The secret of good repointing is to keep the mortar off the face of the brickwork. Take great care when forcing mortar into the joints, removing any excess immediately before it dries.

- Let the joints harden a little before you give them a profile.

- Clean all bricklaying tools immediately after use with clean water. They will be much more difficult to clean if the mortar is allowed to dry.

REPOINTING BRICKWORK

1 Use a thin-blade plugging chisel with a club hammer to free loose mortar from the joints.

2 Brush out dust and debris from the joints and dampen the existing mortar with water.

ABOVE The causes of cracked pointing should be investigated immediately and repaired.

3 Hold the hawk tightly against the wall and push mortar into the joint using a trowel.

4 Give the mortar the profile you want – here, a concave profile using a length of hosepipe.

REPAIRING CONCRETE AND ASPHALT DRIVES

There are many materials that can be used for surfacing paths, patios and drives, and in time most will need some form of repair or maintenance. The technique required depends on the material. Keeping paths, patios and drives in good condition is not simply a matter of appearance. If the surfaces are allowed to deteriorate, they can become dangerous to walk on, especially when wet.

DAMAGED CONCRETE

Concrete is a popular choice for paving because it is relatively cheap and easy to lay. Nevertheless, it can crack, develop holes and crumble at exposed edges.

Before carrying out any repairs to concrete paving, it is a good idea to clean it thoroughly, and the best way of doing this is to use a pressure washer, which directs a high-velocity jet of water at the surface, removing all algae, slime, dirt and debris. Chip out any damaged areas until you have a solid surface to work on.

Minor holes and cracks can be repaired with exterior filler, quick-setting cement or mortar made with fine sharp sand rather than soft builder's sand. However, you should chip out holes to a depth of about 20mm (⅜in) and enlarge cracks to allow the repair compound to grip properly. Any repairs involving edges will require the use of timber shuttering to contain the repair compound while it dries. Fitting shuttering is fairly simple, using stout timber boards. Solid timber pegs are driven into the ground so that the boards fit tightly against the edge of the existing concrete.

Spread the repair compound over the damaged area – some PVA adhesive (white glue) brushed over the surface will help it stick – and smooth it out with a trowel.

Before the repair compound sets completely, roughen the surface with a stiff brush, as smooth concrete

REPAIRING A CONCRETE PATH

1 Clean the damaged path with a pressure washer to remove all dirt and algal growth.

2 Fit a piece of shuttering to the edge of the path and drive the pegs home to hold it.

3 Mix up the concrete repair compound in a bucket with a small amount of water.

4 Use a plasterer's trowel to apply the concrete right up to the existing edges.

surfaces are dangerous when wet. Finally, remove the shuttering and smooth off any rough areas with the trowel and a piece of sacking.

Apart from brushing, there are several ways you can make a concrete surface more attractive and less slippery. Embedding small stones in the surface is one method, or you could provide surface texture with a float or by rolling a heavy pipe over the concrete.

5 Remove the shuttering once the repair compound has dried.

Repairing asphalt

Asphalt (tarmacadam) is an economical and hardwearing paving material. Provided it has been laid properly, an asphalt path or drive can last a long time. After all, it is basically the same material, small stones mixed with liquid bitumen, that is used for making roads.

However, many domestic asphalt paths and drives may have been laid badly and may start to crumble. If weeds begin to break through the surface, it is a sign that an insufficient thickness of asphalt has been laid, and the only sensible answer is to have a second layer professionally installed on top of the existing one. Laying a complete asphalt drive, which needs to be done with hot asphalt, is not a job for the amateur. However, small holes can be readily mended.

The first step is to sweep the existing drive thoroughly, paying particular attention to the area around the intended repair. If the surface adjacent to the damage has become distorted, you may be able to reshape it by heating the surface with a hot-air gun and tamping the asphalt down with a piece of wood.

Cold-lay asphalt repair compounds are normally laid after the application of a coat of bitumen emulsion.

Compact the repair compound into the hole or depression, using a stout piece of wood or a garden roller for a large area. Spray the roller with water to prevent the repair compound from sticking to it. If you want, scatter stone chippings over the asphalt and roll them in.

For really deep holes, it is best to fill them partially with concrete before adding the final layer of cold-fill compound.

Repairing an asphalt path

1 Brush the damaged area of the path or drive until you have a clean working area.

2 Apply asphalt repair compound and press it into the damaged area with a spade or trowel.

3 Tamp the filled area with a stout piece of wood or use a garden roller to flatten it.

4 If required, add stone chippings and then roll again.

Good drainage

If there are puddles forming on your paving or if rainwater does not clear away, it is a sign that the paving has not been laid to the correct slope (fall).

This does not need to be huge and around 1 in 100 is normally recommended, that is 1cm per metre (⅛in per 4ft).

The fall can be checked using a straight timber batten set on edge with a small block of wood under its lower end and a spirit level on top. The thickness of the wood block depends on the length of the batten; for a 3m (10ft) batten, you need a 30mm (1¼in) block.

Safety first

Many paving materials, especially paving slabs, are heavy and have rough edges. So it is important that you wear the correct safety gear – stout gloves and safety shoes as a minimum. Gloves will also protect your hands when using heavy hammers. If you are not strong enough, do not attempt to lift paving slabs by yourself as you could damage your back. Take care, too, when using tools such as angle grinders for cutting paving slabs to fit in corners and other awkward areas.

REPAIRING SLAB AND BLOCK PAVING

Concrete paving slabs are a common choice of paving for patios. The same slabs can also be used for paths, but for drives, stronger and thicker, hydraulically-pressed slabs must be laid on a much stronger base. Normally, paving slabs are set on dabs of mortar on a sand base, but they may also be laid on a solid bed of mortar, a method that is always used when laying heavy-duty slabs for a drive.

REPAIRING SLAB PAVING

A slab may have broken because something too heavy has been placed on it or as a result of something hitting it. Sometimes, individual slabs may become loose or may sink, in which case they will need to be lifted and re-laid.

If the joints around the slab have been filled with mortar, the first job will be to chip this out, using a narrow-bladed masonry chisel.

If possible, remove a broken slab from the centre, working outward; you can use a bolster chisel or a garden spade to lever up sections or whole slabs, but protect the edges of adjoining slabs with pieces of timber. Clean out the bottom of the hole, removing all old mortar, and level it using builder's sand tamped down with a stout piece of wood – allow about 10mm (⅜in) for the mortar. Mix up a batch of mortar

using dry ready-mix and put down five dabs, one in the centre and one near each corner. Also lay a fillet of mortar along each edge.

Lower the new slab, or the old slab if it is undamaged, into position and tap it down with the handle of a club hammer. Check that the slab is level with its neighbours by placing a spirit level across them. Adjust as needed, then when perfectly level fill the joints with more mortar.

REPLACING A CONCRETE SLAB

1 Use a narrow-bladed masonry chisel to chip out the mortar around a damaged paving slab.

2 Lift or lever out the broken pieces, starting from the centre. Clean out the hole.

3 Add more sand and put down five blobs of mortar and apply mortar to the edges.

4 Lower the paving slab into position and make sure it lines up with surrounding slabs.

5 Use the handle of your club hammer to tap the slab into place until it is exactly level.

6 Add some more mortar to finish the joints, smoothing it down level with the paving.

ABOVE Crazy paving paths can be both functional and attractive.

CRAZY PAVING

This form of paving employs pieces of real stone or broken slabs (whole slabs of real stone are prohibitively expensive) and is popular for paths, although larger areas may also be paved in this manner. It can be laid in one of two ways: on a bed of sand or a bed of concrete. Like full-size paving slabs, individual pieces may break, sink or work loose.

When repairing crazy paving, you may need to re-lay quite large areas. As when laying new crazy paving, work from the sides toward the centre, using the biggest pieces with the straightest edges along the sides, then filling in with smaller pieces.

Whichever way you lay crazy paving, the joints should always be well mortared, and the mortar finished flush or shaped with a pointing trowel to give V-shaped grooves around the slab.

REPAIRING BLOCK PAVING

Concrete blocks are also commonly used for paving: the individual blocks are bedded in a layer of sand and held tightly against one another by edging blocks or restraints set in mortar. Fine sand is brushed into the joints between blocks.

If an individual block becomes damaged, the main problem will be getting it out to replace it. Drill holes in it with the largest masonry drill you own, then break it up with a cold chisel and club (spalling) hammer. In this way, you will reduce the risk of damaging the surrounding blocks. Loosen the sand at the base of the hole and add a little more so that the new block sits proud of the surface by around 10mm (⅜in). Tap it down with the handle of the club hammer, then force it into its final position by hitting a stout piece of wood laid over the block with the head of the hammer. Brush fine joint sand into the cracks.

REPLACING A DAMAGED BLOCK

ABOVE A pressure washer is the most effective way of cleaning paving, but you need to be careful not to splash yourself (wear protective clothing in any case) and not to wash earth out of flowerbeds. Never point the spray directly at the house walls.

1 Use a large masonry drill to make a hole in a damaged paving block.

2 Use this hole to start chipping out the block with a cold chisel.

3 Clean up the hole, then add a little more sand to the bottom of the hole.

4 Push the new block into place. Tamp it down, using a block of wood to protect it.

REPAIRING GRAVEL PATHS AND EDGES

One of the big advantages of gravel is that it makes a noise when you walk on it and provides a significant deterrent to potential intruders. It is also good for drives, as it can soak up oil drips from cars without showing permanent stains. However, gravel can become weedy and may blow about. It may also be trodden into the house and develop thin patches.

MAINTAINING A GRAVEL SURFACE

Regular raking and the application of weedkiller are required to keep a gravel drive or path looking good, and you can buy silicone resins that help bind the stones together without affecting their appearance. Thin areas can simply be filled by pouring on a bag of new gravel and spreading it with a garden rake.

To prevent gravel from spreading beyond its allotted area, add concrete edging strips. These should be set on a bed of mortar and held upright while the mortar sets. If you do not like the look of concrete edging, consider using bricks or wood.

You can use the oil-catching properties of gravel to good effect by installing strips of it in a concrete drive where you park the car. The concrete will act to keep the gravel in place and the gravel will catch any oil drips.

To lay a new gravel path, dig out the area, add compacted hardcore, followed by sand and coarse gravel and finally fine gravel to level.

ABOVE Gravels naturally vary considerably in colour and size.

LAYING A GRAVEL PATH

1 Excavate the area to a depth of about 15cm (6in) and make the base firm.

2 Provide a firm edge to retain the gravel. For straight paths, secure battens with pegs.

3 Compact a layer of hardcore. Add a mixture of sand and coarse gravel, and tamp it firm.

4 Top up with fine gravel. Rake and roll repeatedly until the surface is firm and level.

MAINTAINING GRAVEL PATHS

1 Apply weedkiller to a gravel path to keep it looking good.

2 Scatter new gravel on to a path to give it a fresh appearance, and rake it level.

ABOVE This narrow, concrete kerb edging has been used here to contain a gravel garden and to divide it from paving slabs.

ABOVE Handle Victorian-style rope edging carefully if it is made from clay, as it can easily chip or break.

ABOVE Wooden edgings are useful if you want to create a formal or old-fashioned effect. Secure in place with pegs.

REPAIRING EDGING

Edging is an important part of paving, as it can help to hold the main body of paving in place and prevent the edge slabs or blocks from being damaged. There are several kinds, of which the most common are concrete edgings, used with all types of paving, and self-edging where the paving material itself, concrete blocks for example, is used as the edging.

All masonry edging should be bedded in mortar, no matter how the remainder of the paving is laid.

Where edging has become loose, pull it out and chip and scrape away all the old mortar. Lay a bed of fresh mortar and push the edging pieces back into place, using a straightedge to align them with their neighbours. Drive in timber pegs to hold the edging vertical and tight against the paving; finish off by applying a 45-degree fillet of mortar along the base of the edging between the pegs.

When the mortar has set, remove the pegs and make good the peg holes with more mortar and conceal the fillet of mortar with soil or turf.

PRACTICAL TIP

• Paths always make a smarter feature with a neat or interesting edging. If you have an older-style property, try a Victorian-style rope edging. If it is a country cottage, try something both subtle and unusual, such as green glass bottles sunk into the ground so that just the bottoms are visible. Or try bricks: they can be used on their sides, on end, or set at an angle of about 45 degrees.

REPAIRING A PATH EDGE

1 To replace loose edging, the first task is to remove the edging and to clean out all the old mortar, using a chisel if necessary.

2 Push fresh mortar firmly down into the hole, checking that you have enough to bring the edging level.

3 Push the edging piece back into place, lining it up and add an angled fillet of mortar along its bottom edge.

INSULATION AND SECURITY

Insulation helps to protect your home from cold weather by reducing the rate at which expensive domestic heat can escape. As well as insulating your living space, it is essential to provide ventilation – a free flow of fresh air via airbricks and fans. When thinking about doors and windows, always consider security and protection from burglars. There are many locks and bolts that provide an effective defence against unwelcome visitors.

INSULATING ROOFS AND PIPEWORK

Good insulation reduces the rate at which expensive domestic heat escapes through the fabric of your home and helps to protect vulnerable plumbing systems from damage during cold weather. The different parts of your home can be insulated by various methods, and most jobs can be handled by a competent person. The cost will eventually be recouped through savings made on energy bills.

ROOFS AND PLUMBING

As with any do-it-yourself job, breaking the whole project down into manageable parts can help. Around 25 per cent of heat escapes through the roof, so it is a good place to start your insulation project. The roof is where pipework is at greatest risk of freezing, so this must be tackled as well.

SAFETY FIRST

Invest in protective clothing. A basic kit should comprise:
• Well-fitting overalls and gloves to keep out dust particles.
• Protective goggles and face mask.
• A safety helmet, which is essential when working in confined spaces with limited headroom.

Most important of all, remember that unless you have laid suitable flooring in the roof area, you will only be able to walk on the joists. In between will be the exposed ceiling of the rooms below, which will be

RIGHT A cutaway section of a roof showing the roofing felt or building paper, examples of sheet and blanket insulation between the rafters, the vapour barrier and the plasterboard (gypsum board) sheets.

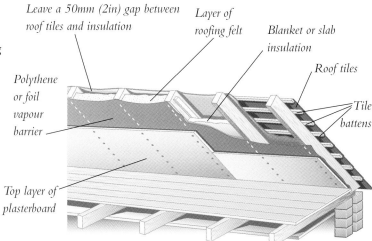

Leave a 50mm (2in) gap between roof tiles and insulation

Layer of roofing felt

Blanket or slab insulation

Roof tiles

Polythene or foil vapour barrier

Tile battens

Top layer of plasterboard

fragile and will not bear your weight. To avoid accidents, lay stout planks of wood across the joists and stand on them.

INSULATION MATERIALS

A simple way to stop heat loss is to place insulation material between the joists. Your choice may be influenced by personal preference or ease of use – some varieties are much cleaner and less likely to cause

skin irritation than others – or the decision may be made for you by the local authority if you are applying for a grant to complete the work.

Current recommendations suggest that the insulation should be laid to a depth of 200mm (8in). However, this may not be possible with some materials if the joists are of a shallower depth. Also, if the roof area has a floor, this may restrict the depth of the insulation. In the latter case, the floor will have to be lifted to put insulation between the joists.

LOOSE-FILL INSULATION

This is sold by the bag and is simply poured between the joists and levelled off with their top surfaces. Although easy to handle and spread, the dustier varieties, such as vermiculite, can be unpleasant to work with. Moreover, the material may be blown about if the roof area is prone to draughts.

LAYING LOOSE-FILL INSULATION

1 Lay loose-fill insulation by pouring the material between the joists.

2 Level off with a spreader, which you can make from a strip of chipboard (particle board).

Blanket insulation

This consists of rolls of glass fibre, mineral fibre or rock fibre, which are simply unrolled between the joists. Widths are available to match common joist spacings. A typical roll length would be 6–8m (20–26ft), but short lengths are also available, known as batts. Some types may cause skin irritation, so always wear gloves when laying the insulation.

Slab insulation

These products are light and easy to handle, but as with the blanket versions some types may cause skin irritation. Again, the slab widths match common joist spacings. Look out for high-density slabs if you want the bonus of an effective sound barrier.

Essential buys

Good insulation need not mean great expenditure. The most effective

Laying blanket insulation

1 Lay blanket insulation by unrolling the material and pressing gently into place.

2 Butt join two rolls of blanket insulation and press the two ends together leaving no gaps.

items are relatively cheap and could save you a great deal in the long term. Any water storage tanks in the roof must be insulated to protect them from freezing; indeed, some water suppliers may require this by law. Padded jackets are available for the purpose. Likewise, any exposed pipework in the roof should be fitted with thick insulating sleeves to prevent freezing.

Practical tips

• Leave the space under a cold-water storage tank free from insulation. Warmth rises from rooms underneath to help prevent freezing.

• Insulate the roof access hatch with blanket insulation, backed with plastic, and glue or pin in place.

ABOVE FAR LEFT Fix reflective foil between rafters to act as a vapour barrier over insulation.

ABOVE LEFT Split foam pipe insulation.

ABOVE Seal pipe insulation with adhesive tape to make it secure.

FAR LEFT Secure an insulation blanket to a hot water cylinder.

LEFT Insulate a cold water cistern with a purpose-made jacket.

INSULATING WALLS AND FLOORS

The walls of any house represent a huge part of the building and it is essential that they are well insulated. The type of insulation required depends on the fabric of your home – solid walls require one method, cavity walls another. It is also imperative to insulate your home at ground level, as around 15 per cent of heat can escape through the floors.

HEAT LOSS IN WALLS

The largest area of heat loss, some 35 per cent, is estimated to escape through house walls. However, the best solution, which is cavity-wall insulation, is a job that must be left to the professionals. Despite the extra outlay, the work is very cost-effective, and you can expect to see a return on your investment after a few years. This treatment, of course, is not possible if the house has solid walls. The usual procedure is to pump foam, pellets or mineral fibres into the cavity through holes drilled in the outer leaf of the wall. Make sure that the work is carried out by an approved contractor.

DO-IT-YOURSELF SOLUTIONS

Applying insulation to the inner faces of walls is well within the scope of most people. One possibility is to use thermal plasterboard (gypsum board) to dry line external walls. Another is to add a timber framework to the wall, infill with slab or blanket insulation and face it with plasterboard. To prevent

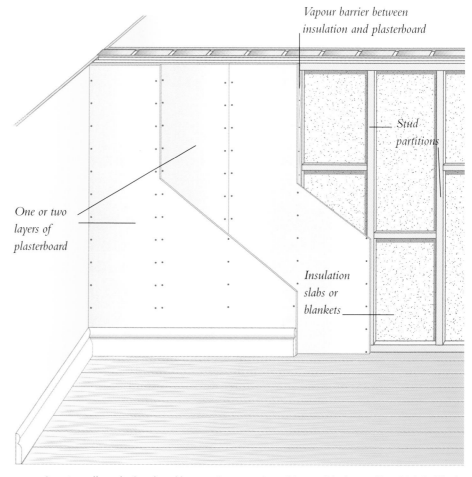

Vapour barrier between insulation and plasterboard

Stud partitions

One or two layers of plasterboard

Insulation slabs or blankets

ABOVE A party wall can be insulated by erecting a stud partition wall in front of it, which is filled in with blanket or slab insulation behind it and two layers of plasterboard on the framework.

condensation, plastic sheeting should be stapled to the insulating material.

The disadvantage of both of these methods is that you will lose some of the floor area of the room. At least 50mm (2in) will be lost by using thermal plasterboard, and more if you create a new partition wall. However, in terms of comfort and cost-savings, this sacrifice may be worth making. Providing the plaster wall is sound, the boards can be fixed directly to it with adhesive. A vapour barrier is included as standard.

ABOVE Installing cavity wall insulation is a specialist job that can take up to three days.

PRACTICAL TIPS

• Fabric wallcoverings have good insulation properties. Similarly, rugs and wallhangings can keep heat in and reduce sound levels.

• Use acoustic slabs when dry-lining walls for a quieter life.

DRAUGHTY FLOORS

If you draughtproof floorboards that have substantial gaps, bear in mind that it could involve disruptive work and should be avoided if possible. If you are prepared to lift and replace floorboards, the methods are very similar to laying roof insulation.

However, you will need to provide some means of supporting the insulation material between the joists. Nylon netting stapled to the sides of the joists is the usual method for holding glass fibre insulation blanket in place. Pull up the netting tightly before nailing down the boards so that the blanket does not sag and let cold air through. Lengths of wood fixed between the joists will support slab insulation.

An easier method of coping with a draughty floor is to choose a good underlay for your carpet and also repair any gaps or cracks between floorboards with sealant.

Larger gaps will need to be filled with strips of wood, carefully cut to fit tightly. Spread adhesive on the sides of each strip and tap it into the gap. Allow the glue to set, then plane down the strip so that it is flush with the surrounding floor.

Solid concrete, or direct-to-earth, floors are generally insulated by covering the area with sheets of rigid polystyrene, topped by a covering of polythene sheeting.

RIGHT Putting aluminium foil behind a radiator will help to save energy by reflecting heat back into the room.

FAR RIGHT Stop draughts at skirting (base) board level by sealing any gaps with mastic and quadrant (quarter-round) moulding. Secure the latter to the skirting with pins.

FILLING GAPS IN FLOORBOARDS

1 Tap slivers of wood in place to cure floorboard draughts. Leave the repair slightly proud of the surface.

2 Once the glue has set, sand down the raised area to a smooth finish with a power sander or planer.

A floating floor, comprising of tongued-and-grooved chipboard, is then installed over this.

A gap of 9mm (⅜in) should be left between the chipboard and the wall to allow for expansion. This gap will not be noticeable once a new skirting (base) board is installed. The layer of air trapped under the floating floor will help keep the area warm.

This work can be fairly disruptive, and as the new floor will be at a raised level, existing doors will need to be removed and planed down. Architraves (trims) around doors will also need to be shortened to accommodate the change.

PRACTICAL TIPS

• Position a shelf about 150mm (6in) above a radiator to project heat into the room.

• A papier-mâché mix made from pieces of newspaper and a thick solution of wallpaper paste can be used to repair small holes in floorboards. Add woodstain to match the surrounding boards, and then sand the repair smooth when dry.

• If floorboards are in very poor condition, cover the area with panels of hardboard or plywood.

DRAUGHTPROOFING DOORS AND WINDOWS

The smallest gaps and cracks in the fabric of your home can create the most uncomfortable living conditions. About 15 per cent of heat loss is attributed to poor or non-existent draughtproofing, yet fitting draughtproofing materials is quite easy and inexpensive. Effective draughtproofing not only stops heat from escaping, but also makes your home feel warmer by eliminating cold draughts.

A HEALTHY BALANCE

The main targets are windows, doors, chimney flues and the roof access hatch, but check also for gaps around skirting (base) boards and between floorboards. However, there is a healthy balance to be struck. If every draught is eradicated, you could create ideal conditions for condensation. The solution is to draughtproof all the obvious cold spots in your home, but also ensure that there is adequate ventilation, in the form of grilles, airbricks and extractor fans.

DOORS AND WINDOWS

These are the two main sources of draughts in the home, and many products have been designed to deal with the problem. Windows alone are responsible for about 10 per cent of heat loss. One solution is to replace single-glazed units with double glazing, but this is the most costly remedy and it may take up to 20 years to recoup your investment in terms of energy savings.

Draught excluder strips are an inexpensive method of sealing gaps around windows and doors. The strips are self-adhesive and easy to apply, although foam strips offer variable levels of success. Avoid the

CLOSING HOLES

Draughts may not only pass around doors, but also through them. The problem is quite easy to solve. Keyhole covers are inexpensive, while a brush-type or rubber flap fixed to the inside of a letter plate will prevent anything other than the mail coming through.

ABOVE Fit a letter box with a rubber or brush seal to stop draughts.

ABOVE A simple cover plate, or escutcheon, will stop draughts.

brush strip

V-strip metal draughtproofing strip

LEFT A metal draughtproofing strip can be fixed to a door frame, such as the example shown here, a V-strip type. The insert shows where the brush strip should be fixed.

BELOW Various types of threshold draught excluders. Most, with the exception of flexible strip excluders, are made for internal or external doors, so choose the correct size and type for your doors.

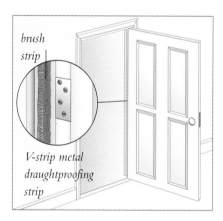

Flexible rubber strip held in place by screws.

An aluminium flexible arch excluder.

Brush-type strip fitted at the base of the door.

All-in-one door kit, with a trim to expel rainwater, plus a draught excluder.

cheapest varieties, as they may soon become compressed and will not do the job properly. Look for products that are guaranteed for between two and five years. These will be easy to remove and replace if you wish to upgrade the draughtproofing system.

Rubber strips, commonly with E- or P-shaped profiles, are dearer, but are better in terms of performance and longevity. Normally, casement windows are easier to draughtproof than the sash variety.

The most effective way of keeping draughts out at the sides of sashes is to fix nylon pile brush strips to the window frame. The top and bottom do not need special treatment, as any of the products recommended for casement windows can be used.

Silicone sealants (caulking) are good for filling large or irregularly shaped gaps around windows and doors. They come in white, brown and clear versions. Use a caulking gun for ease of application, although products that do not require a gun are also available. To make a repair with silicone sealant, clean the frame rebate (rabbet) and apply the sealant to the fixed frame. Brush soapy

water on to the closing edge of the window or door. Close and immediately open the door. The soapy water acts as a release agent, preventing the door or window from sticking to the sealant.

SECONDARY GLAZING

This is a relatively inexpensive way to prevent draughts from windows. The cheapest method involves attaching a clear film to the inside of the window with tape. It can be discarded during the summer months and a fresh film applied in winter.

A sturdier option is acrylic sheet. If you opt for this method, make sure that at least one window is easy to open in case of an emergency.

Alternatively, you could buy a kit that allows the secondary glazing units to slide along a track.

ABOVE Apply sealant to a window.

ABOVE To apply secondary glazing film, stick double-sided adhesive to the frame, fix the film in place and heat it to iron out wrinkles.

PRACTICAL TIPS

• For good adhesion, always clean and dry window and door frames thoroughly before applying self-adhesive sealant.

• Consider adding trickle ventilators to windows to allow essential air into your home.

• When replacing windows, consider using panes of low-emissivity glass. This has a special coating that reflects heat back into the room and gives the same advantages as triple glazing, but for less money.

INSTALLING A RIGID GLAZING SYSTEM

1 Cut the channelling to fit the four edges of the glass or plastic sheet. Fix on to the sheet.

2 Hold the glazing over the window and mark the positions for the fixing holes.

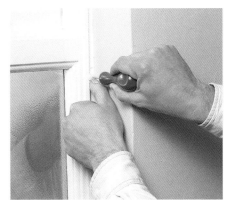

3 Deepen the marked spots with a bradawl to provide pilot holes. Screw the glazing in place.

Providing Ventilation

Ventilation, a free flow of fresh air, is essential in a home, not only for humans to breathe, but also to prevent condensation occurring. There are three main areas of a home that need ventilation: the main living space, the spaces under suspended timber floors, and the roof space. You may also need to ventilate chimneys that have been sealed.

Ventilation for living

In older homes, there are likely to be so many gaps around doors and windows and through fireplaces that any additional ventilation will be unnecessary, although you may need to open a few windows from time to time. In modern homes, the combination of draughtproofed windows and doors and sealed or non-existent fireplaces means that some kind of additional ventilation is necessary. This may take the form of forced ventilation, through an extractor fan in a bathroom or kitchen, or background ventilation, for which the main item is the trickle ventilator.

A trickle ventilator allows a slow, but constant, stream of fresh air into a room and is simply fitted into a window frame. Holes are drilled through the frame and the ventilator fitted over them, thus allowing air to flow into and out of the room. A grille prevents insects from getting in, and there is usually some kind of control to vary the rate of flow.

Underfloor ventilation

A suspended timber floor consists of floorboards or sheets of flooring-grade chipboard (particle board) supported on joists. To keep the joists and the flooring dry, and so avoid rot and woodworm attack, some kind of underfloor ventilation is essential. This takes the form of airbricks fitted in the outer walls.

The first thing to check is that all the existing airbricks are free of debris and have not been blocked up in the mistaken belief that this will save money on heating.

Next, check that there are enough airbricks – there should be one airbrick for every 2m (6ft) of wall length. Inserting a new airbrick is not difficult, as most match the size of standard bricks.

Decide where you want to put it, drill out the mortar around the existing brick and remove it. With a cavity wall, the most common, you will have to continue the hole

through the inner wall and fit a terracotta liner to maintain the airflow. Use the corners of the hole in the outer wall to line up and drill four holes in the inner wall, then chip out the hole with a bolster (stonecutter's) chisel and club (spalling) hammer, working from the inside. You will need to lift floorboards to do this.

Fit the airbrick from the outside, applying mortar to the bottom of the hole and the top of the brick, pushing mortar in the sides. Point the mortar joints to the same profile as the surrounding joints. Mortar the liner in place from inside the house.

Ventilating roof spaces

If your house has a gable end wall, the roof space can be ventilated by fitting airbricks in the gable. If the house is semi-detached, ask your neighbour to do the same, and fit another airbrick in the party wall to allow the air to circulate freely.

Clearing an airbrick

Practical tip

• Where a room contains a gas boiler, current regulations may mean that you need an unobstructed ventilator fitted in an outside wall. Check with your gas supplier (or heating installer) whether you need to have one of these fitted.

ABOVE Airbricks can get blocked by soil, leaves or stones from nearby paths.

ABOVE Clear any debris around the airbrick and clean the holes with a vacuum.

The alternative is to fit ventilators in the timber soffits – the horizontal boards that overhang the eaves. All that is needed to fit these is to cut a hole in the timber using a padsaw or a jigsaw (saber saw), then push the ventilator in place, securing it with screws if necessary. There must be a clear space above each ventilator for air to flow into the roof, so make sure that any insulation material does not extend to the eaves. A badly ventilated roof space can lead to condensation and possible rot.

BLOCKED FIREPLACES

If a fireplace has been bricked or boarded up, the result could be condensation within the old chimney, leading to staining of the chimney breast (fireplace projection) especially if there is no airbrick.

Fit a metal ventilator to the bricks or panel where the fireplace used to be, after making a hole just smaller than the ventilator area. Some types are made to be screwed in place; others, for use with bricks, are held by plaster. If the chimney pot itself has also been removed and the chimney capped off, make sure that airbricks have been fitted into the chimney at the top.

PRACTICAL TIP

• You may need to install more airbricks in a room where there is a solid concrete hearth (from an old cooking range, say). This can create "dead" areas which may need extra ventilation to prevent rot.

FITTING AN AIRBRICK

1 Airbricks are the same size as one, two or three bricks. To fit one, start by drilling a series of closely-spaced holes through the joint around a brick.

2 Then use the club (spalling) hammer and a wide bolster (stonecutter's) chisel to cut out the brickwork. With solid walls, drill holes right through and work from inside too.

3 Fit a cavity liner through to the inner wall if the wall is of cavity construction, then trowel a bed of fairly wet mortar on to the bottom of the opening.

4 Butter mortar on to the top of the airbrick and slide in place. Push more mortar into the gaps at the sides and pack it down. Use drier mortar to point neatly all around the airbrick.

5 As an alternative to the traditional terracotta airbrick, fit a two-part plastic version. The sleeves interlock to line the hole as the two parts are pushed together.

6 Slide the outer section into place, and point around it. Slide the inner section into place from the inside of the house. Fit its cover grille.

FITTING AN EXTRACTOR FAN

If the basic ventilation measures have been undertaken, such as installing trickle ventilators and airbricks, and condensation is still a problem, the answer is to fit an extractor fan. These can be incorporated into walls, windows and ceilings and have the advantage that they get rid of moist and stale air from close to where it is produced.

PROVIDING EXTRA VENTILATION

An extractor fan provides positive ventilation where it is needed, in a kitchen, bathroom or toilet, removing stale or moist air before it can cause a problem. There are three places you can fit an extractor fan: in a window, in a wall and in the ceiling, where ducts carry the stale air to the outside. In a kitchen, an extracting cooker hood can serve the same function, provided it is ducted to the outside; a recirculating cooker hood only filters the air.

It is important that an extractor fan is positioned so that the replacement air, which normally will come through and around the door leading to the remainder of the house, is drawn through the room and across the problem area. In a kitchen, the problem areas are the cooker and the sink; in a bathroom, they are the toilet and shower unit.

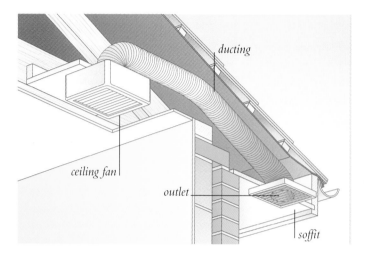

ducting

ceiling fan

outlet

soffit

LEFT Fit an extractor fan in the ceiling so that it discharges via a duct to a hole with an outlet at the soffit.

WINDOW FANS

If a simple window ventilator already exists in a fixed window, you may be able to replace it with an extractor fan. If not, you will have to cut a hole in one of the window panes. However, this will not be possible if the glass is toughened or laminated. The same applies to double-glazed units; they must be ordered with the hole pre-cut. The only window you can cut a hole in is one made from normal glass in a single-glazed frame, and even here you may prefer to order a new pane from a glass supplier with the hole already cut. That way, the only work you will have to do is to take out the old pane and fit the new one.

To cut the hole in the glass yourself, you will need a beam circle cutter as well as a normal glass cutter. Use the beam cutter to score two circles: one the correct size for the extractor fan and one slightly smaller inside it. Then use the normal glass cutter to make cross-hatched lines inside the inner circle, and single radial lines between the two circles. Tap out the glass from the inner circle, then use the glass breaker rack on the glass cutter to snap off the remaining margin of glass. Smooth the edge with fine abrasive paper wrapped around a circular tool handle or piece of thick dowelling rod. Once you have a hole of the correct size, fitting a window

FITTING A WINDOW FAN

ABOVE If no ventilator is fitted, you will need to cut a hole in the glass to fit an extractor fan.

ABOVE If the window already has a simple ventilator, remove this to fit an extractor fan.

fan is simply a matter of following the instructions.

WALL EXTRACTOR FANS

Most designs of extractor fan will require a circular hole to be cut through the house wall. The best tool to use for this is a heavy-duty electric drill fitted with a core drill bit, both of which you can hire. This will cut a hole of exactly the correct size. Make holes in both leaves of a cavity wall and fit the sleeve supplied with the extractor fan. Some fans require a rectangular hole to be cut, which may mean removing a whole brick. Fitting the fan is easy – simply drill holes for wallplugs to take the fan on the inside wall, and fit the outlet on the outer wall.

CEILING FANS

A wall outlet for the ducting from a ceiling fan is fitted in the same way as for a wall extractor fan. It is often the easiest type to fit, as all you need to do is cut a circular hole in the ceiling with a padsaw, taking care to avoid the ceiling joists. From the fan, plastic ducting needs to be taken to an outside wall or to the eaves, where it is connected to an outlet. At the eaves, it is fitted into the soffit in the same way as a soffit ventilator.

WIRING

An extractor fan needs to be wired up via a fused connection unit to the nearest power supply circuit. If you are not sure how to do this, employ a qualified electrician to do the job. In a bathroom, or room containing a toilet, with no opening window, a fan is a compulsory requirement and it must be wired via the light switch so that it comes on with the light and remains on for 15 minutes afterwards.

FITTING A WALL EXTRACTOR FAN

1 The first step in fitting a wall fan is to mark the exact position of the wall sleeve.

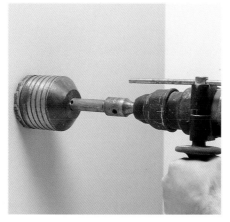

2 Use a core drill bit (with a heavy-duty drill) to cut a hole of the correct size.

3 Fit the sleeving right through the wall, cutting it to the correct length if required.

4 Drill holes for wallplugs so that you can screw the extractor fan to the wall surface.

5 Wiring comes next (get help with this if necessary), after which the cover is put on.

6 Finally fit the outlet on the outside wall (sometimes this just pushes into the sleeve).

DAMP AND CONDENSATION

This can ruin decorations, destroy floorcoverings, damage walls and plaster, and cause woodwork to rot, so it is important not only to treat the symptoms, but also to track down the causes. These could vary from rain coming in through the roof or walls, condensation, moisture being absorbed through the ground or a mixture of these.

PENETRATING DAMP

This is caused by moisture getting in from the outside, often because of wear and tear to the structure of your home, but it may also affect solid walls that are subjected to strong driving rain. The first sign of penetrating damp appears after a heavy downpour and can occur almost anywhere, although it may be some distance from the actual leak; mould often forms directly behind where the problem lies.

CAUSES OF PENETRATING DAMP

- Damp on ceilings upstairs may be caused by broken or loose roof tiles, or damaged copings.
- Damp on a ceiling spreading from a chimney breast (fireplace projection) or rooflight, under the junction of two pitched roofs, or in corners that adjoin a single-storey extension, is usually caused by flashing that has parted company with masonry, or cracked and crumbling mortar fillets.
- When damp patches are high up

on an upstairs wall, look for blocked, defective gutters or downpipes and a build-up of leaves.
- With widespread damp on a wall, look for cracked or porous bricks.
- Isolated damp patches on walls are caused by crumbling pointing and cracked or blown patches of render (large damp patches), or mortar-encrusted wall ties (small spots).
- Rotten woodwork and damp patches around door and window frames are caused by gaps between masonry and frames, missing weatherboard or a drip groove encrusted with paint or moss.

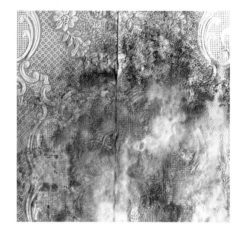

ABOVE LEFT A patch of mould on the inner face of an external wall is usually the first sign of penetrating damp.

ABOVE Poor ventilation will make condensation problems worse.

BELOW FAR LEFT Crumbling mortar and defective flashing can cause penetrating damp.

BELOW LEFT Overflowing or broken gutters allow water to seep through masonry.

BELOW A defective roof leaking through cracks and gaps and soaking structural timbers will cause major problems, such as damp, wet rot and dry rot.

Rising damp

This is caused by water soaking up through floors and walls, and is usually confined to a 1m (3ft) band above ground level. It is a constant problem, even during dry spells.

The main areas to check for rising damp are the damp-proof course (DPC) around the foot of walls, and damp-proof membrane (DPM) in the ground floor. Older properties were often built without either, which can lead to widespread damp. If existing materials have broken down or structural movement has caused defects, there may be isolated, but spreading, patches of damp where water is penetrating. A DPC that is less than 150mm (6in) above ground level will allow rain to splash above it and penetrate the wall, which may cause damp patches at skirting (base) board level. If a DPC has been bridged, either by exterior render or interior plaster, there will be damp just above skirting level. A cavity filled with rubble, soil or plants growing against the wall may also allow damp to penetrate.

Condensation

When warm, moist air reaches a cold surface, such as a wall exposed to icy winter winds or ceramic tiles,

the result is condensation. It is most likely to occur in bathrooms and kitchens where the main activities are bathing, washing and cooking. Controlling condensation requires a fine balance between good ventilation and adequate heating, but while the modern home is warm, it is also well insulated and draughtproofed, so the level of ventilation is often poor. The key to success is to provide sufficient ventilation, without allowing expensive heat to escape.

BELOW LEFT Water vapour from everyday activities can cause condensation.

BELOW Condensation is feature of our modern well-insulated and draughtproofed homes, but keeping it under control is essential to the health of your house and family.

ABOVE LEFT Gaps between masonry and woodwork around windows will let in rain, causing patches of damp to occur.

ABOVE Injecting an interior wall with silicone – you will need to get professional help to do this.

Is it damp or condensation?

If you are not sure if a moisture problem is due to condensation or damp, lay a piece of aluminium foil over the patch, seal the edges with adhesive tape and leave it for 48 hours. Condensation will cause beads of moisture to appear on the surface of the foil; penetrating or rising damp will produce beads of moisture underneath the foil.

ABOVE Test with aluminium foil to determine whether the problem is damp or condensation.

Overcoming Damp and Condensation

Damp and condensation should never be ignored, as these unchecked problems will not go away and may well indicate more serious problems. Often the remedy is quite straightforward and inexpensive, but the after-effects can linger for some time, and then real effort is required when it comes to cleaning up and making good afterwards.

Damp-proof courses

The first line of defence against damp is an effective damp-proof course (DPC) combined with a good damp-proof membrane (DPM), backed up by well maintained rainwater systems and plumbing. Ventilation is the key to preventing condensation problems. An adequate airflow should be maintained through the fabric of the house, using soffit vents and airbricks, while extractor fans will deal effectively with the warm, moist air created by everyday activities such as cooking, laundry and bathing.

Dealing with damp

Once the cause of penetrating damp has been traced and repaired, the problem will be eradicated. The remedy for rising damp caused by a non-existent or defective DPC or DPM is not so easy; the only solution is to install a replacement or make thorough repairs.

ABOVE A damp-proof course should be clear of soil, debris or plants growing up walls.

Waterproofing walls with water seal

1 Brush, clean, and remove any fungal growth from the wall. Fill any surface cracks.

2 Apply the water seal by brush, working from the bottom up, coating the whole wall.

However, dealing with a DPC that has been bridged is quite straightforward. If the ground level is the cause, digging a 150mm (6in) wide trench between a high patio or path and the house wall, then filling it with gravel, will allow rain to drain away more rapidly. When you suspect that debris in the cavity, or a dirty wall tie, is the cause, removing a few bricks will give access to remove the rubble, or chip away encrusted mortar. Apply a coat of liquid water repellent to the area once the bricks have been replaced.

The after-effects

Walls and floors can take up to a month for each 25mm (1in) of thickness to dry out, while old plaster may be heavily contaminated with mineral salts from rising damp, which will continue to absorb moisture from the air. Replastering is recommended in extreme cases as part of the cure, but this should be delayed for as long as possible to allow walls to dry out. Use a mould killer to remove any patches of mould from interior surfaces caused by damp or condensation.

Damp-proof courses

There are many ways of installing a damp-proof course, ranging from physical DPCs that are cut into the brickwork to chemical slurries, which are pumped into a series of drilled holes.

In theory, it is possible to do the job yourself, but dealing with rising damp is rarely simple. It is worth seeking the advice of professionals. If there is a mortgage on your home, the lender may also require a guarantee of workmanship, which rules out tackling the job yourself. The standard of workmanship is as important as the system used, so choosing a reputable company that offers an insurance-backed guarantee is essential and often compulsory.

INSTALLING A DAMP-PROOF MEMBRANE

This is a job that a competent do-it-yourselfer can tackle. Laying a new damp-proof membrane (DPM) involves digging up and re-laying the old floor slab, which is hard work, but the most effective method of damp-proofing a concrete floor. A floor can also be damp-proofed by applying several coats of moisture-curing urethane, but it is essential that any leaky patches are sealed completely first with a hydraulic cement.

A third option is to apply two coats of rubberized bitumen emulsion to the old surface, then cover this with a cement-sand screed, which will raise the level of the floor by about 50mm (2in).

Whichever method you choose, the DPM material should be taken up the adjoining walls to meet the DPC, if there is one. The problem of damp floors caused by rising ground-water levels, which typically affects basements, is more serious and requires structural waterproofing or "tanking", which is certainly a job for the professionals.

COPING WITH CONDENSATION

Steam from cooking can be removed by a fully vented cooker hood, but where a great deal of steam is produced, when you take a shower for example, the best way to remove it is with an extractor fan.

To be quick and efficient, the fan must be sited properly and it should be the correct size for the room. In a kitchen, a fan must be capable of ten to 15 air changes per hour, and in bathrooms six to eight air changes per hour, which should be increased to 15 to 20 air changes for a power shower. Simply multiply the volume of the room by the number of air changes required and look for a fan that offers the same cubic metre/foot capacity per hour (m³/hr/ft/hr).

An extractor fan should be installed as high as possible on the wall, and as far as possible from the main source of ventilation, usually diagonally opposite the main door is ideal.

More widespread condensation can be alleviated with an electric dehumidifier, or prevented with a thermostatically controlled whole-house ventilation system.

ABOVE A cooker hood removes steam from cooking at source.

PRACTICAL TIPS

• In bathrooms, keep the door shut when taking a bath and run cold water first to minimize the amount of steam it creates.

• Where condensation occurs in a confined space, such as a built-in wardrobe, causing mould and mildew, use silica gel crystals to absorb excess moisture from the air.

• In kitchens, make sure a tumble drier is properly vented.

INSTALLING A DAMP-PROOF COURSE

1 A chemical damp-proof course is injected into a line of drilled holes about 115mm (4½in) apart.

2 Once injected into the drilled holes, the chemicals overlap to form a continuous impermeable barrier.

3 When the fluid is dry, the drilled holes are filled with mortar and then a rendered surface can be painted.

WOODWORM, DRY ROT AND WET ROT

Rot and woodworm are the enemies of timber and every homeowner's nightmare, yet by taking a few simple steps both can be prevented. In addition, once discovered, repair can often be a do-it-yourself proposition. At the first sign of infestation, act quickly and try to identify and eradicate the problem before it seriously damages your home.

WOODWORM

This mainly affects structural woodwork, such as roof timbers, staircases, floorboards and joists, and unprotected parts of furniture, such as drawer bases and the backs of cabinets. It will also attack plywood and wicker.

The most common menace is the furniture beetle, whose larvae create fine boreholes 1–2mm (1/16in) in diameter. Larger holes are likely to be caused by the house longhorn

PREVENTATIVE ACTION

• Inspect all second-hand furniture before buying, and treat with woodworm fluid before bringing indoors, whether it shows signs of infestation or not.

• Protect unpainted wood, the top and bottom edges of doors for example, with insecticide.

ABOVE Check your furniture, and if necessary, treat it with a proprietary woodworm fluid.

beetle larvae, which prefers softwood and creates boreholes 3–6mm (1/8–1/4in) in diameter, and the deathwatch beetle larvae, which makes substantial boreholes and has an appetite for structural timbers.

It is possible to treat infestation in furniture and localized outbreaks in structural timbers with woodworm fluid, but if the wood is crumbling, the only remedy is to remove and replace the affected areas.

Woodworm fluid will not penetrate a polished surface, so treat boreholes with an aerosol spray or nozzle applicator. Boreholes are connected by a series of tunnels, so you only need to do this every 75mm (3in) or so. Leave the timber to dry for at least 24 hours and then wipe off any excess.

Seek professional help to deal with a large-scale infestation, or if it has compromised the strength of structural timbers.

ABOVE Woodworm can be identified by tiny holes. Check the extent of the infestation by inserting a knife into affected timber.

WET ROT

This thrives on wet timber and frequently appears where timber is close to the ground or near leaking plumbing, and in woodwork where the protective paint coating has broken down. Skirting (base) boards may also be affected where a DPC is defective or non-existent.

Wet rot can be due to a number of species of fungus, but the most common consist of brown or black strands that appear on the surface, causing the wood to crack and eventually disintegrate. Affected wood tends to look darker than healthy wood and feels spongy.

Once the cause of the damp conditions that have led to the problem is eliminated, wet rot fungus will die. Treat small areas, such as window frames, with proprietary wood hardener solution and insert preservative tablets into holes drilled into the wood to stop

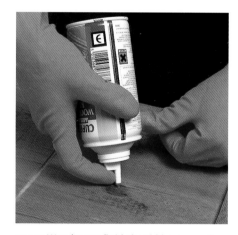

ABOVE Woodworm fluid should be sprayed on to all surfaces of structural timbers. On small areas, apply two coats of woodworm killer.

any recurrence. Where damage is extensive, the affected wood should be cut out and renewed.

DRY ROT

The fungus that causes dry rot loves moist, humid conditions and has a taste for resins and silicones in untreated wood. However, the grey strands are fine enough to penetrate masonry, which means that it can spread rapidly from room to room.

Untreated dry rot will destroy floors, doors and skirtings, and infect plaster and ceilings. Initially, it manifests itself as a brownish-red dust, but within days the spores will have developed into a fungus that looks like a mushroom growing upside-down and it also gives off a distinctive musty smell. This is the final stage of germination, by which time the fungus will be producing millions of spores to infect surrounding areas.

Dealing with dry rot is a job that should be entrusted to a specialist, as it may recur if not treated properly. Make sure you choose a reputable company that offers an insurance-backed guarantee.

ABOVE An example of severe dry rot on a destroyed wooden floor.

ABOVE A sporophore, or dry rot fungus, on a structural roof timber.

ABOVE Inspect your loft space and check for the first signs of dry rot. Ensure there is good ventilation in the loft and under the floors to help prevent the conditions in which dry rot can flourish.

PREVENTATIVE ACTION

• Make sure that a damp-proof course (DPC) has not been bridged, by looking for tell-tale signs of damp on walls above skirtings.

• Dry rot will not flourish in well-ventilated areas, so make sure there is good ventilation in roofs and under suspended wooden floors. If necessary, fit air vents or extractor fans in soffits and gable end walls. Make regular checks of the airbricks and clear them if they are blocked.

PRACTICAL TIPS

• Make regular checks of plumbing, especially under baths and shower trays and in the roof.

• Many of the chemicals used to treat woodworm and dry rot are flammable or toxic irritants, which create strong fumes that will linger for about a week. This means taking precautionary measures for at least two days after treatment.

REPLACING ROTTEN WOODEN SILLS

1 Remove the rotten wood and cut a new wedge-shaped piece to fit.

2 Fix the new wood in place by countersinking the screws.

Home Security

Most burglars are opportunists, and will take a chance if they spot a property that looks as if it offers quick and easy takings. The golden rule is to leave your home as secure as possible whenever you go out. Protecting your home from unwelcome visitors does not have to be difficult or expensive; often the simplest measures are the most effective.

Locks and bolts

The first line of defence is to make sure that all windows and doors are adequately protected with good-quality locks and bolts. Surface-mounted locks and bolts are easy to install, but fittings that are mortised into the frame are much stronger and more secure. The second line of defence is to make your home less vulnerable and less attractive to opportunist burglars.

Cylinder rim lock

Double-barrel cylinder lock

High-security cylinder deadlock

Secondary security

Doors

- Locks will be ineffective if a door is flimsy or ill-fitting, and a well-fitting, solid wood or blockboard door, at least 44mm (1¾in) thick, offers the best resistance.
- To prevent a door from being lifted off its hinges, fit security hinges, which have lugs that will not come apart if the hinge pin is removed. If the door opens outward, fit hinge bolts.
- For personal safety when you are home, a door viewer will allow you to decide whether or not to open the door to a caller. Choose a

High-security cylinder sash lock

Five-lever mortise deadlock

viewer with a wide angle of vision, and use it in conjunction with a porch light. You should be able to see someone who is standing to one side of the door, or crouching below the viewer.

- A door chain will give added protection against forced entry. Its effectiveness will depend on how well it is anchored to the door and frame: use the longest and heaviest-gauge screws that you can.

ABOVE Fit hinge bolts to doors that open out.

ABOVE Check out callers with a door viewer.

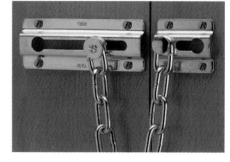

ABOVE Prevent forced entry with a door chain.

Patio doors

- Sliding patio doors are a favourite point of entry, so fit anti-lift devices as well as locks to prevent the doors from being lifted from their tracks.
- A locking bar across the full width of the door will create an immediate, visible deterrent to potential intruders.

Windows

- If casement windows are not fitted with trickle vents or locking handles, replacing the stays with locking stays will provide more security when leaving the windows open for ventilation.

SECURITY SYSTEMS

A burglar alarm may also deter a thief from choosing your home. Installing a do-it-yourself system is time-consuming rather than difficult, but you should be able to install a wireless alarm in about four hours and a wired system in one or two days. Some wireless systems are not completely wire-free, as the control panel has to be wired to the alarm siren on the outside of the house. However, the latest solar-powered alarm systems have an external siren that has its own integral trickle-charge battery, so that no wiring is required.

Basic alarm kits offer rudimentary protection, so additional components will be needed to provide adequate security. This increases the cost, but do-it-yourself systems nevertheless offer good savings over a professionally installed system. If you cannot afford an alarm system, a dummy alarm box fitted outside may make a burglar think twice.

PROTECTIVE MEASURES

Glass

- Laminated or toughened glass will make it difficult for a burglar to break in without creating a lot of noise. It may be worth replacing glass panels in vulnerable doors and windows.

Lighting

- Replacing an existing light switch with a photocell switch that will turn lights on at dusk, and off again after a pre-set interval, will keep a potential burglar guessing whether you are in or out. A light that can be programmed to switch on and off at random is convincing.
- Exterior security lights that switch on automatically when movement is detected nearby are also a powerful deterrent in dark areas around your home.

LEFT A security light that will automatically illuminate when someone approaches is an ideal choice for front doors.

BELOW LEFT A passive infra-red detector can be used to monitor a dark passageway or the back yard or garden, turning security lights on automatically when movement is detected.

BELOW A security camera with a built-in passive infra-red detector will detect and record movement, indoors and out.

PRACTICAL TIPS

- Outbuildings and garages should always be locked securely. Not only are they a source of easy takings for a thief, but the ladders and tools inside are perfect implements for breaking into your home.

- Large hedges can screen doors and windows and provide burglars with enough privacy to break in undetected by neighbours, so keep them well trimmed.

- Make vulnerable corners of the garden more secure by planting dense, thorny evergreens. A liberal layer of gravel under windows makes a quiet approach to the house impossible.

WINDOW HARDWARE AND LOCKS

Over half of all home burglaries occur through a window and even the smallest one is vulnerable, so good locks are very important. The first line of defence is to fit key-operated locks to all ground floor windows, and those first floor windows that are easily accessible. It is also essential to provide secure ventilation around your home.

BASIC HARDWARE

The most common items of hardware fitted on hinged windows are a rotating cockspur handle that is used simply to fasten the window, and a casement stay which props it open in one of the several different positions. On sliding sash windows, the basic hardware is a catch that locks the two sashes together when they are closed.

WINDOW LOCKS

A wide range of locking devices for windows is available. Many are surface-mounted using screws and are quick and easy to fit, although for some types a drilled hole for a bolt or recess chiselled for a keeper plate may be required. Mortised locks and dual screws that fit into holes drilled in the window frame take longer to install, but they are very secure.

All window locks are supplied with fixing screws but these should often be discarded in favour of longer, more secure fixings. For extra security, it is also a good idea to fit two locks on casement windows more than 1m (3ft) high and all locking devices for sash windows are best used in pairs.

For ventilation, if the window has a stay pierced with holes, you can replace the plain peg with a casement stay lock. Attach the screw-on lock to the threaded peg with the key supplied. You can now secure the window in position.

FITTING A WINDOW HANDLE AND STAY

1 Choose the position of the cockspur handle on the casement and make pilot holes through it with a bradawl. Then screw the handle to the casement.

2 Fit the striking plate (keeper) to the frame so that it will engage with the cockspur. Drill out the frame to a depth of 20mm (¾in) through the slot in the plate.

3 Fit the casement stay by screwing its base-plate to the bottom rail of the casement about one-third along from the hinged edge.

4 Open the window to find the right position for the pins on the frame. Attach the pins, then fit the stay rest on the casement rail.

If fitting lockable window catches and stays, do not leave keys in the locks where they might be seen by an intruder or in case they fall out as the window is opened and closed. Instead, hang them on a hook close to the window.

PRACTICAL TIP

• Ensure you have the right screws: a lock for wooden frames requires wood screws and metal windows require self-tapping screws.

CASEMENT LOCKS

Locks for wooden casement windows may be surface-mounted or set in the frame. In the former case, the lockplate is attached to the fixed frame and the body of the lock to the opening frame. With the window closed, mark the positions of the lock and plate on both frames, then screw them in place. For those with a locking bolt, you will have to cut a rebate (rabbet) or drill a hole to receive the bolt. Some surface-mounted locks are also suitable for metal casement windows. Check the instructions.

Locks that are set in the frame normally require holes to be drilled in both fixed and opening frames. Also, a hole must be drilled through the face of the frame for the key.

SASH LOCKS

Some types of casement-window lock will also work with sash windows. Another option is key-operated dual screws, which bolt both sashes together. Use a flat bit the width of the lock barrel to drill through the inner meeting rail into the outer rail to the required depth, then tap the barrels into place with a hammer and piece of wood. Fit the longer barrel into the inner rail, the shorter into the outer rail, and screw the bolt into the barrel with the key.

FIRE SAFETY

Wherever possible, fit window locks that all use the same standard key so that any key can be used to open a window in the event of an emergency. Keep the key in an accessible position.

FITTING A CASEMENT LOCK

1 With the lock assembled, mark the position on the fixed and opening frames.

2 Separate the two parts of the lock and screw the body to the opening frame.

3 Fit the cover plate and insert the screws. You may want to use longer screws.

4 Some makes come with small covers to hide the screws. Tap these into place.

FITTING A SASH WINDOW LOCK

1 Mark the drill bit with tape to the required depth and drill through the inner meeting rail of a sash window and into the outer rail.

2 Separate the two sections of the lock and tap the barrels of the dual screw into place in the meeting rails (mullions).

Door Locks

Doors, especially those at the rear of the house, often provide an easy entrance and exit point for intruders. Good locks properly fitted to a strong door and door frame are the basic requirements for ensuring that house doors are secure, while additional security devices may help you feel safer at home. The doors of garages and outbuildings are also at risk and need to be protected too.

Installing mortise locks

Align the mortise lock with the centre rail of the door and use the lock body as a template for marking the top and bottom of the mortise.

Draw a line down the middle of the door edge and, using a drill bit the width of the lock body, drill a series of overlapping holes along the centre-line to the depth of the lock. Chisel out the mortise so that the lock body fits snugly. Insert the lock, mark the outline of the faceplate with a marking gauge and chisel out a recess so that it fits flush with the door edge.

Mark the positions of the key and spindle holes, then drill them using a twist drill of the same diameter; enlarge the keyhole with a padsaw. Assemble and check the lock works.

With the latch and bolt open, mark their positions on the door frame. Measure from the outside of the door to the centre of the bolt, mark that distance on the jamb and cut mortises in this position. Chisel a recess for the striking plate and check that the door closes properly before screwing it in place.

Practical tip

• "Measure twice and cut once." Accuracy is vital when measuring out for door locks, so take your time with this part of the job and you will have fewer problems later.

Fitting a mortise lock

1 Mark out the dimensions of a mortise lock on the door edge.

2 Draw a vertical line in the exact centre of the door between the marked lines.

3 Drill a line of holes through the centreline to the depth of the lock body.

4 Insert the lock, then mark and chisel out the recess for the faceplate.

5 Using the lock as a guide, mark the position of the spindle and keyhole.

6 Drill, then use a padsaw to form the keyhole, then fit the covers.

7 Cut out mortises for the latch and the deadbolt on the door jamb.

8 Cut out a recess for the striking plate (keeper) so that it fits flush in the door jamb.

FITTING A RIM LOCK TO A DOOR

Mark the position of the lock on the door, using any template provided, and bore a hole with a flat bit for the key cylinder. Push the cylinder into the hole, connect the backplate and secure it with screws. The cylinder connecting bar will protrude through the backplate. If necessary, cut it to length using a hacksaw.

Mark and chisel out the lock recess in the door edge, then fit the lock and screw it to the door, making sure that the cylinder connecting bar has engaged in the lock.

With the door closed, mark the position of the striking plate (keeper) on the jamb, then chisel out the recess so that the plate fits flush with the frame. Fix the striking plate with screws and check that the door closes properly.

FITTING RACK BOLTS

Mark the position of the rack bolt in the centre of the door edge and on the inner face of the door, using a try or combination square to ensure that the two marks are level. Drill horizontally into the door edge to the depth of the body of the bolt.

Push the bolt into the hole, mark the outline of the faceplate, then withdraw the bolt and chisel out a recess for the plate. Hold the bolt level with the guideline on the inside of the door, and mark and drill a hole for the key.

Fit the bolt, following the manufacturer's instructions, check that it works properly and screw the keyhole plate to the door.

Close the door and wind out the bolt so that it leaves a mark on the jamb. Drill a hole at this point and fit a recessed cover plate.

FITTING A RIM LOCK

1 Mark the position of the cylinder on the door and drill its hole.

2 Insert the barrel of the cylinder into the drilled hole.

3 Fit the backplate to the door and secure it tightly with screws.

4 Mark the length of the connecting bar to be cut off if necessary.

5 Fit the lock case on to the connecting plate and screw up.

6 Mark the position of the striking plate. Chisel out the wood to fix to the frame.

FITTING A RACK BOLT

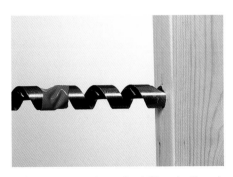

1 Use tape to mark out the drilling depth and keep the drill bit horizontal. Push in the bolt.

2 Mark the outline of the faceplate then withdraw the bolt to chisel out the recess.

GLOSSARY

Architrave (trim) A type of timber moulding, used mainly around openings in walls for doors.

Batten (furring strip) A name given to a straight length of timber, used for temporary or permanent support e.g. of roof tiles, wall tiles or for setting concrete.

Bevel An angled edge on, for example, a piece of wood. Also see *chamfer*. Also a carpenter's tool for setting an angle.

Bolster (stonecutter's) chisel A flat-bladed chisel used for cutting masonry. Used widely by electricians, plumbers and paving contractors; can also be used for levering up floorboards.

Butt joint A joint between two pieces of timber when one piece simply meets the other, such as in an L-shape or a T-shape or end-to-end.

Casement window A window which is hinged at one side or at the top.

Caulking gun A device for squeezing sealant or adhesive out of a cartridge.

Centre point The sharp point of a twist drill bit or a metal plug put into a dowel hole to transfer its position to a second piece of wood.

Chamfer An angled edge to timber, usually smaller than a *bevel*.

Chipboard (particle board) An inexpensive manufactured board consisting of timber scraps and glue.

Clearance hole A hole drilled to take the full size of a screw.

Consumer unit The modern term for an electrical fuse-box. It may contain miniature circuit breakers rather than fuses depending on its age.

Combination ladder A ladder that can be used in two or more ways. Uses include: step-ladder, straight ladder, stair ladder and extending ladder.

Cornice, Cove (crown molding) A decorative timber, plaster or polystyrene (styrofoam) moulding to cover up the join between wall and ceiling.

Damp-proof course An impermeable layer put in exterior walls to prevent damp rising up the wall.

Damp-proof membrane An impermeable layer put in floors to prevent damp rising.

Depth stop A device attached to an electric drill to limit the depth of a hole being drilled.

Door furniture A general term for the bits screwed on to doors, such as handles, knockers and knobs.

Duckboard A low slatted timber platform for standing on.

Eaves A general term for the wood pieces where the roof meets the house walls. Consists of *soffit* and *fascia board*.

Fascia (board) The vertical timber boards at the *eaves*. Gutters are usually fixed to these.

Fillet A thin narrow strip. Usually applied to strips of mortar used in paving.

Flashing Strips cut from lead or zinc sheet used to seal roofing junctions.

Float glass The modern replacement for sheet glass and plate glass (so called because in manufacture it is floated out of the furnace on molten tin).

Fungicide A chemical treatment for removing mould and algal growth.

Fused connection unit An electrical fitting allowing electric equipment to be permanently wired in.

Gable The pointed walls, sometimes found at the ends of a pitched roof.

Galvanized Coated with zinc to prevent steel from rusting.

Grain The texture of timber created by the annual growth of a tree.

Handed Refers to hinges (e.g. rising butt hinges) attached to either the right or the left of the door.

Hardcore A mixture of stones and rubble used to provide a base for paving and concrete.

Joists Large pieces of timber used in house construction to support floors, ceilings and flat roofs.

Lath-and-plaster An old-fashioned way of constructing ceilings and partition walls. The plaster is applied to thin timber strips (laths), which are secured to vertical studs (walls) or horizontal joists (ceilings).

Leaded light A window where small panes of glass are held between lead strips.

Mastic (caulking) A non-setting and flexible waterproof sealant.

MDF Medium-density fibreboard. A manufactured board consisting of timber fibres and resin. Has smooth surface and will take screws and nails, but needs handling with care.

Mitre A joint made by cutting two pieces of wood at 45 degrees, such as for making picture frames.

Mortise A deep slot cut in timber, for example, for a mortise lock. A mortise chisel is a strong type for levering out the wood.

Oilstone A flat abrasive stone used with oil for sharpening chisels and knives.

Overflow An essential part of a sink, basin or bath or a pipe attached to a water tank.

Party wall The wall between two semi-detached houses or two terraced houses.

Pilot hole A small hole drilled to guide a larger drill or to take the point of a screw that then cuts its own thread.

Pitch The slope of a roof or a staircase.

Planning permission Local authority consent needed in the UK and other countries to build a house or for certain extensions and alterations.

Plasterboard (gypsum board) Sheets consisting of solid plaster contained by heavy paper sheets, used for constructing partition walls and ceilings.

Plywood A man-made board consisting of thin sheets glued together. Alternate sheets have the grain running at right angles giving it exceptional strength.

ACKNOWLEDGEMENTS

Pointing Using extra mortar to finish the joints between bricks in a wall.

Punched Applied to nail heads to mean that they are pushed below the surface of timber with a nail punch.

PVA (white) glue Strictly polyvinyl acetate: a type of adhesive used for wood-working, also used in concreting work to reduce the absorbency of surfaces.

Rebate (rabbet) A slot cut out of the corner of timber to hold something.

Render A mixture of sand and cement used to coat external walls.

Residual current device An electrical safety device that prevents electric shock.

Reveal The rectangular hole in a wall in which a window or door is fitted.

Rim lock (rim latch) A lock (or latch) that is attached to the surface of a door unlike a *mortise* lock, which fits into a slot cut out of the door.

Rising butts Hinges that lift a door as it is opened.

Router An electrical woodworking tool that cuts a slot or a recess.

Sash A name for a window, usually applied to sash windows where each window slides vertically.

Shuttering A framework of timber boards used to hold concrete while it sets.

Silicone A flexible non-setting plastic used in sealants.

Skew (toe) nailing Driving nails in at an angle to provide a stronger bond.

Soffit The horizontal timber boards used at the *eaves*.

Soil pipe The large vertical drainage pipe in houses taking the toilet waste.

Stopcocks Valves fitted to water pipes to stop the flow of water through them.

Trap A device fitted in the waste pipe under a bath, basin or sink to prevent foul air and small animals getting in.

Waste Material that is cut off and not used.

Waste pipe The pipe taking dirty water from bath, basins, sinks and showers.

The publisher would like to thank the following for permission to reproduce their images in this book:

Axminster Power Tool Centre: 15bc; 16tc; 50tr. **Junckers**: 6c. **Fired Earth**: 7br. **DIY Photo Library**: 12bl, br; 13bl, c, br; 42–3 all; 44–5 all; 63cl; 72br; 81bc; 83bl, br. **John Freeman**: 84bl. **Simon Gilham**: 61bl; 76bc, br; 80bl, c, br; 82bc; 83tr; 85bc, br; 87. **HSS Tool Hire**: 16c; 17t, c, r; 83bc. **Rentokil**: 81tr; 85tc, c, tr. **Thompson's (Ronseal)**: 82tc, tl. **Yale Security Products**: 86.

The publisher would like to thank the following for their help with photography and images:

Axminster Power Tool Centre
(see Suppliers)

Burlington Slate Limited
Cavendish House
Kirkby-in-Furness
Cumbria LA17 7UN
Tel: 01229 889661

Canonbury Art Shop
266 Upper Street
London N1
Tel: 020 7226 4652

Colour Centre
(see Suppliers)

David Cropp
Rentokil Initial plc
East Grinstead
West Sussex RH19 2JY
Tel: 01342 830220
http://www.rentokil-initial.com/photos

Dewalt Power Tools

Eternit Building Materials

Heward and Dean (BD) Ltd
(see Suppliers)

Hunter Plastics Limited
Nathan Way
London SE28 0AE
Tel: 020 8855 9851

Marley Roofing Products

Mr. Mark Blewitt
c/o The National Federation of Roofing Contractors

Plasplugs Ltd.
(see Suppliers)

Sandtex
Julie Coleman
ICAS Public Relations
19 Garrick Street
London WC2E 9BB
Tel: 020 7632 2424

Thompson's
Pure PR
PO Box 1430
Sheffield S11 7XH
Tel: 0114 230 9112

Vallance Adhesive and Sealant Range
Stransky Thompson PR
Denton House
40–44 Wicklow Street
London WC1X 9HL

Vitrex Limited
(see Suppliers)

Yale Security Products UK Limited
Wood Street
Willenhall
West Midlands WV13 1LA
Tel: 01902 366911

Suppliers and Useful Addresses

United Kingdom

Axminster Power Tool Centre
Chard Street
Axminster
Devon EX13 5HU
Tel: 01297 33656
Power tools supplier

Black and Decker and Dewalt
210 Bath Road
Slough
Berkshire SL1 3YD
Tel: 01753 567055
Power tools supplier

Colour Centre
Offord Road
London N1
Tel: 020 7609 116
Paints and DIY equipment supplier

Foxell and James
Farringdon Road
London EC1M 3JB
Tel: 020 7405 0152
Wax, oil, varnish, and finishing products.

Heward and Dean
Grove Park Road
London N15 4SP
Tel: 020 8800 3447
Tool supplier

HSS Power Tools
25 Willow Lane
Mitcham
Surrey CR4 4TS
Tel: 020 8260 3100

James Latham
Leeside Wharf
Mount Pleasant Hill
Clapton E5
Tel: 020 8806 3333
Timber suppliers

Plasplugs Ltd.
Wetmore Road
Burton-on-Trent
Staffordshire DE14 1SD
Tel: 01283 530303
www.plasplugs.com
Tiling tools, fixings and fasteners

Record Tools Ltd.
Parkway Works
Kettlebridge Road
Sheffield S9 3BL
Tel: 0114 244 9066
Hand tools supplier

Ronseal Limited
Thorncliffe Park
Chapeltown
Sheffield S35 2YP
Tel: 0114 246 7171
www.ronseal.co.uk
Ronseal, Colron, Thompson's products

Spear & Jackson
Neill Tools Ltd.
Atlas Way
Atlas North
Sheffield S4 7QQ
Tel: 0114 261 4242
Tools supplier

Stanley Tools UK Ltd.
Beighton Road East
Drakehouse
Sheffield S20 7JZ
Tel: 0114 276 8888
Tools supplier

Vitrex Ltd.
Everest Road
Lytham St. Annes
Lancashire
FY8 3AZ
Tel: 01253 789180
Tools and clothing

Woodfit Ltd.
Kem Mill
Whittle-le-Woods
Chorley
Lancashire PR6 7EA
Tel: 01257 266421
Furniture fittings supplier

United States

Compton Lumber & Hardware Inc.
P.O. Box 84972
Seattle, WA 98124-6272
Tel: (206) 623-5010
www.comptonlbr.com

Constantine's
2050 Eastchester Road
Bronx, New York NY 10461
Tel: (718) 792-1600
www.constantines.com

The Cutting Edge, Inc.
7123 Southwest Freeway
Houston, TX 77074
Tel: (981) 9228
www.cuttingedgetools.com

**Northern Tool and Equipment
Corporate Headquarters**
2800 Southcross Drive West
Burnsville, MN 55306
Tel: (800) 533-5545
www.northerntool.com

AUSTRALIA

BBC Hardware Stores
Hardware House
For details of your nearest store
in either of the above two chains,
contact (02) 9876 0888.

Mitre 10
For details of your nearest store
contact (03) 9703 4200.

Bunnings Warehouse
For details of your nearest store
contact (03) 9607 0777.

Thrifty-Link Hardware
See your local state directory for
your nearest store.

USEFUL ADDRESSES

British Cement Association
Century House
Telford Avenue
Berkshire RG45 6YS
Tel: 01344 762676
www.bca.org.uk

**British Wood Preserving and
Damp-proofing Association**
1 Gleneagles House
Vernon Gate, South Street
Derby DE1 1UP
Tel: 01332 225100
www.bwpda.co.uk

**Conservatory Association/Glass
and Glazing Federation**
44–48 Borough High Street
London SE1 1XB
Tel: 01480 458278
www.ggf.org.uk

Energy Saving Trust
21 Dartmouth Street
London SW1H 9BT

Tel: 08457 277200
www.est.org.uk

Home Energy Efficiency Scheme
Eaga Partnership
2nd Floor, Eldon Court
Eldon Square
Newcastle-upon-Tyne NE1 7HA
Tel: 0800 316 6011

Kitchen Specialists Association
12 Top Barn Business Centre
Holt Heath
Worcester WR6 6NH
Tel: 01905 726066
www.ksa.co.uk

Laminated Glass Information Centre
299 Oxford Street
London W1R 1LA
020 7499 1720
www.martex.co.uk/prca/condor

**National Association of Loft
Insulation Contractors**
and
**National Cavity Insulation
Association**
PO Box 12
Haslemere
Surrey GU27 3AH
Tel: 01428 654011
theceed@computer.com

National Fireplace Association
6th Floor
The McLaren Building
35 Dale End
Birmingham B4 7LN
Tel: 0121 200 1310

**RIBA (Royal Institute of
Chartered Architects)**
66 Portland Place
London W1B 1AD

Tel: 020 7580 5533
www.architecture.com

**SALVO
(Directory of Salvage Yards)**
PO Box 333
Cornhill on Tweed
Northumberland TD12 4YJ
Tel: 01890 820333
www.salvo.co.uk

**The Association of Noise
Consultants**
6 Trap Road
Guilden Morden
Hertfordshire SG8 0JE
Tel: 01763 852958
www.association-of-noise-
consultants.co.uk

**The Institute of Electrical
Engineers**
2 Savoy Place
London WC2R 0BL
Tel: 020 7240 1871
www.iee.org.uk

The Institute of Plumbing
64 Station Lane
Hornchurch
Essex RM12 6NB
Tel: 01708 472791
www.plumbers.org.uk

INDEX